I Will Carry You Through: Finding Hope for The Wounded Soul.

Anne Loïs

DISCLAIMER

The experiences and reflections shared in this book are deeply personal and represent the author's journey and perspective.

This book is not intended as professional advice, whether medical, psychological, or otherwise, but rather as an invitation to reflect on one's own story and spiritual journey.

These stories, which include moments of depression, low self-esteem, etc. are shared with hope and the intention of offering comfort to those who may relate.

Readers are encouraged to seek appropriate support and guidance for their unique circumstances.

The names, details, and events in this book

may have been changed to protect the privacy of individuals involved.

Any resemblance to actual people, living or deceased, is coincidental unless explicitly stated.

The author wishes to honor diverse perspectives and experiences and does not intend to minimize or undermine cultural values or individual beliefs.

DEDICATION

To God,

who is the source of all inspiration and strength — this work is for Your glory.

You have been my everything:

a loving Father, a wise Counselor, and, most of all, a faithful Friend.

With You, I can be honest and unguarded, knowing I am fully seen, fully known, and fully loved.

I approach You with boldness, free from fear, always embraced in Your boundless love.

Thank You for being my guide, my comfort,

and my anchor throughout this journey.

To myself,

for starting something and seeing it through to the end – a first and a milestone I will always treasure.

I am proud of the perseverance and courage it took to complete this work,

and I celebrate this achievement as a reminder of what is possible.

I cannot wait to see what else God has in store for me

on this incredible journey.

PREFACE

When I began writing this book, it was never intended for the world to see. It started as something intimate, a secret journal meant only for me and my future daughter. I wanted to leave her a legacy, a guide to help her navigate life; to share the lessons I've learned through the many challenges and victories I've faced. I imagined that one day, when she was ready, I would hand her these words—quiet, personal, and full of the wisdom that I had gathered along my journey.

But as I wrote, something unexpected happened. I felt a stirring in my heart, a call that I could not ignore. What started as a private letter for one, I began to realize, was meant for many. God impressed upon me that my journey—though filled with pain, doubt, and searching—could be a source of light for others. It wasn't just my future daughter who could benefit from these reflections; there are countless people walking through their own storms, questioning their purpose, and struggling to find meaning in their pain.

This book, then, is no longer just a legacy for my future daughter. It is a gift for you, the reader, whoever and wherever you are. My hope is that through these pages, you will find new meaning in your own story. That you'll begin to see that, even in the darkest moments, God's hand has never been far away. That His presence, though sometimes hidden by the fog of our struggles, has always been near, guiding, shaping, and redeeming every part of our journey.

I understand how easy it is to turn from God when tragedy strikes. To question His goodness when life seems anything but good. I've walked through those valleys myself, and I know the weight of those doubts. But through it all, I've discovered a truth that I want to share with you: as long as you are alive, your story is not done. The trials, the heartaches, and even the failures are not the end. There is always more ahead, more growth, more healing, more purpose.

This book is an invitation to look back over your life, to ask the tough questions, and to seek God in the places you least expected Him to be. It is my prayer that as you do, you'll find a renewed sense of hope and purpose. You'll begin to see that the seemingly random events of your life have been woven together with intention, each thread contributing to the masterpiece of your story.

So, as you read, I pray that your heart will be open to discovering God's presence in your life—perhaps in ways you've never considered before. May you be reminded that, no matter how difficult the journey has been, God has always been with you, and He is not done with your story yet.

This is my offering to you, with the hope that it will inspire, encourage, and uplift you. Because if there's one thing I've learned, it's that even in our brokenness, God is crafting something beautiful.

INTRODUCTION

Pain has a way of distorting our vision, clouding our ability to see God clearly. When tragedy strikes, it becomes easy to blame Him and ask, "If God is so good, why would He allow this to happen?" The confusion only deepens when what we know about God does not seem to match the harsh reality through which we are living. In these moments, we may wonder, "Where is God in all this?" or "Why is He silent when I need Him the most?"

This book invites you to take a step back and ask those difficult, yet necessary, questions: "God, where were You when this happened? Where are You now?" It challenges you to search for His hand, not just in the joyful, peaceful times, but also in the pain, the silence, and the unanswered questions. It is in the midst of struggle, when the world feels darkest, that our deepest transformations often take place.

I have not written this book in traditional chapters but in sections. Each section begins with a piece from my personal journal—words I never intended to fit into this book, yet they belong here. These journal entries serve as a guidepost, helping you understand the direction each section will take, as they reflect my raw, honest reflections during the moments of my life when I was searching for meaning.

Additionally, most of the events in this book are not always presented in chronological order. Instead, I've arranged the chapters in a way that provides a sense of continuity to the overall narrative, allowing the themes and reflections to flow more naturally.

Also, at the end of every section, you will find a Bible verse and some reflection questions. I learn best when I am able to put what I have learned into my own words and meditate on it—my hope is that it will be the same for you. Use it to write your own thoughts, your own story of pain, suffering, or wherever you have seen God's hand in your life.

This book is not just about my journey; it is about yours as well.

My hope is that through my story, you will begin to see your own. Perhaps you will realize that everything you have been through has not been in vain, and that there is meaning in your pain. Even if you feel that your burdens are too big to be understood by anyone, remember this: God understands. He knows you intimately, and He desires good things for you, even in the midst of your hardest moments.

There is a song that comes to mind whenever I walk through my own valleys, and its words bring me comfort when I feel overwhelmed:

> *"I do not move by chance; I have a Creator who desires good for me.*
>
> *Lord, You know me—my beginning and my end. What should I fear?*
>
> *In the furnace, I walk unharmed; in the desert, I see Your hand.*

The lion's mouth closes before me, thanks to the God of hope."

Though I have forgotten the source of this song, its message has stayed with me. I pray that its words will resonate with you as you journey through this book, and that they will provide encouragement for you in your own battles.

As you read these pages, I want you to know that your pain is not meaningless. The events of your life, even the hardest ones, are threads being woven into the fabric of your story—perhaps to help someone else, or perhaps to shape you into the person God has always intended you to beloved, valued, and cherished.

You are not forgotten, and your story is not over. There is a purpose behind each trial, and though you may not see it now, each struggle is forming you, preparing you for something greater.

When you pass through deep waters, they will not sweep over you, because God is with you (Isaiah 43:2-3a). Even in suffering, you are not alone. My prayer is that, as you walk through these difficult moments, you will discover not only who you were meant to be but also who God truly is—faithful, loving, and ever-present. His hand is always there, even when it is hard to see, guiding you, protecting you, and carrying you through.

May this book be a reminder that, even in silence and in suffering, there is hope. May you find that hope, and in it, find the strength to keep moving forward.

You were always there

When I look back on this journey, through the trials I have survived,

I see your hand in every moment, guiding me with love and light.

And if I ever get there, Lord, it was you and not me,

Your grace has been my anchor, freeing my spirit.

May I never forget where you brought me,

From the shadows to the dawn, where your mercy shone.

May I never try to usurp your glory and act as if it were all mine,

For every victory, every step is a testimony of your divine.

In the moments of deepest darkness, when I stumbled when I fell,

You lifted me up with kindness, whispered truths to me that time would tell.

And if success finds me, may my heart forever see,

It was your power; it was your wisdom that carried me.

In times of temptation, when pride begins to grow,

Remind me of your sacrifice, of the love you always show.

Let humility be my beacon, let gratitude be my song,

Because you are the one who writes my story, it is to you that I belong

And if one day I get there, Lord, it was you and not me,

With a heart of gratitude, I will sing forever.

I.

I cannot precisely pinpoint where it all began, but the memory remains vivid, lodged deep in the recesses of my mind. It was an ordinary evening, and we were all gathered in the living room, my entire family and I. The atmosphere was familiar, comforting, but somehow, it felt different that night. I can't quite recall if my father was there; he wasn't much for television unless a sermon or something spiritually enriching was on.

But that night, we watched "The Passion of Christ," a film that no child, perhaps, should witness at such a tender age. I was no older than ten-Probably Seven or Eight years old.

Now, Let me tell you about "**The Passion of the Christ**." It's a 2004 film directed by Mel Gibson that focuses on the final 12 hours of Jesus Christ's life. The movie portrays, in intense detail, the events leading up to and including his crucifixion. It's known for being very graphic and emotional, showing everything from his betrayal by Judas, his trial before the Roman and Jewish authorities, to the brutal torture and suffering he endured. The film does an incredible job of conveying the physical and emotional pain that Jesus went through.

What stands out is how it shows not just the cruelty and violence of crucifixion, but also the moments of love, forgiveness, and sacrifice. The entire movie is in Aramaic, Latin, and Hebrew, which gives it a very authentic feel, like you're seeing these events unfold as they might have in reality. Some people, including myself, find that movie particularly difficult to watch due to its raw intensity and emotional impact. I was a child—innocent, impressionable. The images on the screen left an indelible mark on my young soul, searing it with a mix of fear, awe, and a deep, unnamable sorrow.

The next day was like any other—or so it seemed. I went outside to play, as children do, in that gentle twilight that softly signals the end of the day. There was a guava tree near our garage, a place I loved to climb, feeling like a conqueror atop my leafy fortress. But that day, something was different. As I approached the tree, I noticed a cord tied there, dangling ominously as if someone had placed it with intent, a silent invitation to something I couldn't yet comprehend.

Side Story:

There was once a family living just behind our house. They had a small boy who often came to play with us, usually when his parents weren't around. I vividly recall the sounds that would echo from their home—raised voices, crashing objects. On those days, the woman of the house would appear at our door, holding her son tightly in her arms, rocking him back and forth, her tears falling silently.

It wasn't until later that I learned the truth. Her husband was a heavy drinker, and when he returned home in one of his dark moods, he would lash out, hitting her without mercy. The child, helpless and frightened, would often be caught in chaos. That's why she ran to our house for refuge, or perhaps my parents brought her over, fearing for her life, worried that if she stayed, the abuse might one day go too far.

I come from a patriarchal culture that significantly elevates men, often turning a blind eye to their faults while holding women to a stringent standard. This cultural framework is steeped in an informal "law" that favors men, granting them leniency for their actions, whereas women face severe consequences for even minor transgressions. For instance, in the case of my neighbor, society would expect her to "be the bigger person"—to endure the pain, suppress her feelings, and accept her situation as a testament to her strength and character. This mentality suggests that true womanhood is defined by one's ability to suffer in silence.

Leaving an abusive relationship is not just frowned upon; it can result in complete social exile. A woman who chooses to leave often faces a stigma that tarnishes her reputation, rendering her an outcast in her community. She becomes a target of scorn and ridicule, treated as if she embodies the worst qualities imaginable. It is heartbreaking to see that there are women within this culture who perpetuate these harmful beliefs, reinforcing the notion that a woman's worth is tied to her endurance of suffering.

An expression that captures this mentality is "Kanga Motema," which translates to "endure." This phrase reflects the expectation that a woman should possess a heart full of resilience and self-sacrifice, often at the expense of her well-being. This cultural narrative diminishes the importance of a woman's happiness and health, instead celebrating her ability to endure hardship and remain silent. This deeply ingrained mindset not only harms individual women but also perpetuates a cycle of suffering that limits both personal growth and societal progress.

Continued:

In my innocence, I didn't recognize that tied cord for what it was—a noose. A tool of despair and finality. Then, out of nowhere, a voice resounded in my head, not my own, but one that felt ancient, authoritative. It whispered, no, it commanded me to hang myself. It promised that all the pain, the confusion, the loneliness that weighed so heavily on my young heart would disappear if I just placed that cord around my neck.

I used to think that the boy had placed that cord there himself, maybe intending to play with it, unaware of the darkness lingering just behind his innocent intentions. Or maybe the woman did, honestly, I am not sure.

I was a child of deep emotions, often overwhelmed by the persistent feeling that I was unloved, unwanted, a burden. The world, I believed, would be better without me in it. So, when I heard that voice, something in me wanted to believe it—to trust that ending it all would bring peace, that it would make everything better.

I moved toward the cord, my small hands trembling. But then, as I reached out, a vivid flashback struck me—a scene from the movie we had watched the night before. Judas, tormented and alone, hanging himself in despair. The darkness that surrounded him, the malevolent spirits that came to claim his soul, it was a terrifying image, one that made my blood run cold. I didn't fully understand it then, but I knew I didn't want to share his fate.

Fear gripped me, pulling me back from the brink. I turned and ran, not stopping until I reached the safety of the big living room, where I found my mother. She was there, praying fervently, her hands resting gently on her swollen belly, cradling the life within. Breathless, I told her what had happened, and she prayed for me. Her words, soft yet powerful, filled the room, and as she prayed, the darkness lifted, replaced by a calm I hadn't known before.

For a moment, I believed that everything would be okay, that the bad feelings would vanish, never to return. But deep down, a part of me sensed that this was only the beginning—the beginning of a journey I was yet to fully understand.

Romans 8: 28

And we know [with great confidence] that God [who is deeply concerned about us] causes all things to work together [as a plan] for good for those who love God, to those who are called according to His plan and purpose'

There are moments in life, like the one I experienced as a child watching *The Passion of the Christ*, that feel overwhelming—too raw, too intense to grasp. At the time, I couldn't understand why something so painful to watch was allowed to touch my heart so profoundly. All I could see was the heaviness of the moment, the weight of emotions I couldn't name or process.

But looking back now, I see it differently. Through the lens of Romans 8:28, I understand that even that moment was part of God's greater plan. What felt like a random, painful experience was actually God at work. Though I didn't yet realize it, His love was already covering me, and His hand was protecting me. God was weaving His plan, ensuring that whatever the enemy intended would not succeed.

The movie wasn't just a film—it was a tool God used to protect me. It left a mark so vivid that whatever the enemy had planned for me the next day was dismantled before it even began. This truth doesn't erase the intensity of what I felt, but it reframes it. It reminds me—and it can remind you, too—that God is always at work, even when we don't understand.

This is the beauty of God's promise in Romans 8:28. He doesn't waste a single experience, no matter how heavy it might feel at the time. The pain, the confusion, the moments that seem too much—all of it becomes part of a greater purpose in His hands. He takes what was meant to harm us and turns it into something that refines us, anchors us, and ultimately works for our good. Even when we don't yet understand His love or His plan, He is already at work, proving His faithfulness.

No matter what you face or how deeply it marks you, trust that God is weaving it all together for your good and His glory. What the devil meant for harm, God transforms into something that shapes us, strengthens us, and leads us closer to His purpose. You are never alone in your struggles, and nothing in your life is wasted in His hands.

Reflection Questions:

1. The cultural concept of "Kanga Motema" emphasizes enduring suffering in silence. Do you find yourself accepting hardship in your own life without expressing your pain? How might this mindset affect your well-being, and what would it mean for you to break that cycle? ? what steps are you willing to take to build a community of people who can uplift and stand by you when you need it most?

2. What would it look like for you to truly believe that you are never alone in your struggles and that God is always weaving your experiences into a masterpiece of redemption? How might that belief impact your daily walk with Him?

3. Think about a time when something you initially saw as harmful or negative turned out to lead you closer to God's purpose. What does this teach you about trusting Him in your current struggles?

4. Take a moment to reflect on how God has already shown His faithfulness in your life. What specific instances come to mind, and how can remembering these moments help you trust Him in the future?

The Misunderstood Woman

She holds the strength of a lion yet the softness of silk—a masterpiece of God, precious and forgotten.

Often mistreated, enduring pain.

She bears the burdens of life without question, Yet, this world judges her harshly, refusing to recognize her worth.

Wife, Mother, sister, daughter—the woman is the very essence of life.

Her strength rivals a thousand warriors, yet she is shackled by customs that don't see her, traditions that erase her identity.

She is lost in a reflection that reveals nothing; her name, her voice, her very being obscured.

She wonders, "Who am I?

Am I the broken image before me, or the silent strength within? Am I a ghost, a forgotten spirit, or a dream longing for freedom?"

Woman, unarmed, unloved, carrying life yet left empty. She gives her all, only to be replaced, her love left unreturned. She becomes a shadow, a flame fading into the past. But woman, you are strong, resilient, a treasure.

Black, white, brown—woman of any color, you are valuable. Your past does not define you. Listen closely: a celebration awaits, a future that honors your strength, your courage, and the enduring beauty within.

Can you hear it?

II.

Culture can leave some deep scars, especially when it gets tangled up with religion in a way that feels more like control than anything else. It's strange how easily faith and tradition can merge, and yet, not always in ways that truly reflect the heart of God.

Now, what I'm about to say might make some people uncomfortable, but this is just my perspective. It's based on my own experiences, and in no way am I claiming this as some divine truth.

I grew up in a world where, as a girl, my worth seemed to hinge on one thing: marriage. From an early age, many girls are taught that their primary purpose is to marry and please their husbands. If you didn't get married by a certain age, it was often seen as a sign that something was wrong with you.

What troubled me even more was the belief, particularly prevalent in my tribe, that women shouldn't prioritize their education. People would ask, "What's the point of schooling if your main goal is to become someone's wife?" This mindset felt incredibly suffocating. While my family didn't impose these views to the same extent, there were still unspoken expectations about the appropriate age for marriage.

The pressure on women to marry at the right time, to have children as soon as possible, and to bear as many as their husbands want—was all so overwhelming to me.

Even worse was the expectation that if your husband cheats and brings children from outside the marriage, you should simply accept it. Society will call you a saint for raising those kids.

But what about the woman who's left to carry the emotional burden? And we're taught that this is just life. That we should prepare ourselves for it so that when it happens, we won't be surprised.

A friend once told me about his uncle who started cheating on his wife because, in his eyes, she wasn't taking care of herself properly. She would wake up and clean the house, make everything ready for him and their kids, but apparently, because she didn't brush her teeth right away, he thought it justified his infidelity. Instead of talking to her or offering any help, his solution was to betray her. And somewhat that was acceptable.

The same goes for domestic abuse. Women are expected to endure it silently, to accept their suffering as part of their duty. I've known women who've stayed in abusive relationships because they were told it was their cross to bear. That was too heartbreaking.

Then there's the whole issue around virginity. I'm not saying women should be careless with sex. I believe it's a sacred act, meant to be cherished within marriage. But what frustrates me is the lack of compassion for women who've lost their virginity, no matter how it happened. Life is messy—some women are raped, others are abused. But what about the girls who, in their innocence, believed that by giving their virginity, they were offering the ultimate gift of love?

Maybe they thought that by doing so, they would secure a man's love, or perhaps it was their way of proving they were enough that he wouldn't need to stray.

But after the painful realization that reality doesn't work that way, they can't go back to the person they were before. Society doesn't see their innocence, their hopes, or the depth of their feelings. All it sees is that they lost something. And they're left to carry that judgment, with no grace in sight.

I'd often wonder why leaders talked so much about the grace of God, about forgiveness, but where was that grace for women? Why were they so quick to judge? Why punish women for circumstances they often can't control or are not taught to prevent? Or maybe the grace of God was not for women?

I remember one story from my childhood that used to haunt me. My mother had a close friend who was killed by her husband. He had forbidden her from going to church, and despite her attempts to negotiate, he remained firm in his decision, but she decided to go anyway. He came home early, found her gone, and waited for her to return. When she did, his anger boiled over. He beat her so badly that she fell, hit her head, and died. What was even more shocking than her death was the way people responded.

They praised her for being a good wife who endured suffering, and some even excused her husband's actions. "She should have just listened," they said. It was like they didn't even care that she had died at the hands of the man who was supposed to protect her.

That's when I realized how deeply ingrained this mindset was. It made me hate my culture for a long time. I didn't want anything to do with it. I struggled to believe that God loved me—or women at all.

It felt like, as a woman, God neither cared for my well-being nor wanted the best for me; instead, I felt cursed to endure a life filled with pain. Reading the Bible only deepened my despair.

Passages like Genesis, which detail the curse on women, left me feeling even more hopeless. As a Christian, I questioned why I should continue to embrace my faith if this is what it meant? I used to dream about running away, about living somewhere far where no one knew me or had any expectations of me. I just wanted to be free—free from the oppressive traditions that defined my worth by my ability to serve a man, to endure, to suffer in silence.

Growing up in that environment twisted my view of God, of men, of society. And, if I'm honest, sometimes it made me want to disappear. The pressure, the expectations, the weight of it all—it was too much. Sure, there are beautiful parts of my culture, but when it came to the way women were treated, I couldn't find peace.

So, I prayed, day after day, that I would one day be free. I had wished things could be different for the women in my culture, the ones who long to be free but felt like they can't. My hope for them was that one day they'll realize there is more to life than simply enduring silently. I dreamed of a world where they didn't have to carry the weight of these expectations, where they could break free from the chains of tradition. A world where they don't have to suffer in silence, but can live fully, freely, and with dignity.

1 Peter 2:9

But you are not like that, for you are a chosen people. You are royal priests, a holy nation, God's very own possession. As a result, you can show others the goodness of God, for he called you out of the darkness into his wonderful light.

In the midst of the pressures and expectations of society, it is easy to lose sight of who we truly are. The world constantly measures our worth against its standards- society's ideals of success, beauty, popularity, and achievement. We are often told that our value is determined by how well we conform to these standards: the careers we build, the relationships we maintain, and the image we project.

It can feel overwhelming to live up to these expectations, and many of us end up questioning our own worth when we fall short of them.

However, the Bible offers a radically different perspective, one that shifts our focus away from societal approval and instead anchors our identity in the unchanging love of God.

Jesus has already overcome the very systems and expectations of the world, and through His victory, we are empowered to do the same. When we place our identity in Christ and understand that He has already conquered the forces that seek to define us by worldly standards, the weight of societal expectations begins to lose its power. We are no longer driven by the need for external validation because we find our worth in the One who created us.

This truth brings freedom — the freedom to be who God has called us to be, regardless of how the world views us. We are not beholden to the shifting norms and fleeting judgments of society. Instead, we are invited to embrace a higher calling, one rooted in God's eternal love and purpose for our lives.

In 1 Peter 2:9, we are reminded of this identity; this passage invites us to see ourselves not as products of society's expectations but as God's beloved and chosen people. Our true worth is not found in meeting the standards of others, but in the fact that we are valued and treasured by God.

We are set apart, called to live with purpose, and empowered to shine His light in a world that often defines success by worldly measures.

When we grasp this truth — that our value comes from God's love and His plan for our lives — the pressure to conform to societal expectations begins to fade. We are free to live as God's special possession, embracing our unique identities and purpose.

Rather than chasing after the ever-changing norms of culture, we are called to reflect God's love and grace, becoming a living example of the truth that our worth is not defined by the world but by the One who created us.

As we lean into this understanding, we are empowered to navigate the weight of societal expectations with grace and confidence, knowing that our true identity is secure in God's hands. This not only frees us but also encourages others to find their worth in Him, helping them see that they, too, are chosen and deeply loved by the Creator.

Reflection questions:

1. Take a moment to reflect on areas in your life where you may feel pressured to meet external standards. How do these pressures impact your self-perception? Do they cause you to question your value? In what ways can you shift your focus from the world's definition of success to God's definition of your worth?

2. Consider the implications of being chosen by God and treasured by Him. How might this affect how you approach your struggles and societal pressures? How can embracing this identity help you find peace, purpose, and confidence despite the pressures to conform?

3. Reflect on specific situations where you find yourself seeking approval or trying to meet external standards. How can you remind yourself that your worth is not defined by others' opinions, but by God's love for you? What practical steps can you take to embrace your true identity in these areas?

4. Think about the times when societal pressures, disappointments, or difficulties have weighed on you. How does Jesus' declaration that He has "overcome the world" change the way you approach these challenges? What would it look like for you to find comfort and strength in His victory rather than in your circumstances?

I dislike the night.

It carries a suffocating weight that's hard to shake.

Often, when I'm inside, it feels as though the walls are closing in on me, pressing in from all sides.

It's as if every sinister force awakens during these hours, targeting me specifically to remind me of my solitude.

There's only me, with no one else to share the burden. The heaviness is almost tangible, like I'm shouldering the weight of the entire world.

It bears down on me relentlessly, and I fear that I might eventually break under pressure.

I have an overwhelming urge to run away and hide, to find some place where I can escape this crushing sensation, but I know I can't.

This oppressive feeling isn't something I can outrun; it comes from deep within me and follows me wherever I go.

Despite this, I have a fervent desire to overcome these emotions.

I want to find a way to confront and dispel the darkness that envelops me each night, to free myself from the internal torment that plagues me.

III.

I was a remarkably interesting child—always in my head, thinking, analyzing, trying to make sense of the world. A detective of sorts, but not the kind you'd expect. I wasn't interested in solving crimes or uncovering secrets about people's day-to-day lives. No, my investigations were much deeper, more abstract, as if the very fabric of existence had handed me a set of clues that no one else could see. I was a detective in pursuit of the meaning of life, of people, of the world itself. God, religion, culture—these were my mysteries, my cases to crack. They fascinated me, but they also overwhelmed me. The vastness of it all intrigued me, yet I was often paralyzed by the enormity of the questions. I was just a child, after all. What could I possibly uncover with such a small, unformed mind? And yet, I couldn't shake the feeling that there was something I needed to understand, a piece of the puzzle I was missing.

This need to understand set me apart from others. It was like being on a different frequency, one where the conversations, the laughter, and the chaos around me were muted, distant. I existed in a parallel world, always peering through the window, trying to connect the dots between what I saw and the deeper reality I felt was out there. Especially in my own family, this difference became more and more obvious as I grew up. My world was one of silence, of careful observation, while the world around me was loud and colorful, filled with noise and activity. I wasn't just quiet—I was a stark contrast to the vibrant, noisy household I grew up in. It wasn't just a personality quirk; it was as if I belonged to a distinct species altogether.

My mom would often tell me that when I was a baby, I was such a good baby—I never gave her any trouble even as a toddler. She would tell me that her and my dad could leave me to my own devices while they spent time together, confident that I wouldn't make a fuss. I imagine they thought I was just easygoing, happy in my solitude, Maybe, even then, I was already lost in thoughts, already wrestling with the questions that would later consume me. I found comfort in being alone, but not because I didn't crave connection—rather, the noise of the world sometimes felt too much to handle. Alone with my thoughts, I could sift through them at my own pace, trying to make sense of things, even if they scared me.

I grew up this way—quiet, introspective, a world of thoughts swirling in my mind, each one chasing after answers that always seemed just out of reach. I would write in my journals, filling page after page with observations, questions, musings about God, life, and the strange workings of the human soul. It was in those pages that I felt most alive, able to articulate the unspoken fears and desires that tangled in my heart. Meanwhile, my siblings lived in a completely different world. They were loud, boisterous, always making a fuss—sometimes even fighting, their laughter and shouts echoing through the house like a constant hum. They were extremely social, thriving in the company of others. It was as if they had some unspoken agreement with the world, an effortless understanding that allowed them to belong without question. They loved to talk, to interact, to lose themselves in stories and games. Hours would pass as they sat around the fire, sharing tales—mostly scary ones, which I found both fascinating and unsettling. I loved to listen, but always from a distance, always on the edge, never fully participating.

I wondered why I couldn't be like them. What was wrong with me? Why did I always feel so different? At first, I thought maybe it was just a matter of time, that eventually, I'd find my place, that I'd grow out of this sense of separation. So, I clung to that hope, keeping my head high, waiting for the day when I would feel like I belonged. But as time passed, that day never came. Instead, I found myself retreating further into my own world, withdrawing from the noise and energy that surrounded me. The gatherings my siblings loved became overwhelming, and while I would participate from time to time, it was always with a sense of distance, as though I was playing a role rather than truly engaging

By the time I reached adolescence, the sense of being different had morphed into something far darker. What had once been a quiet detachment turned into a deep, consuming sense of hopelessness. It was as though a shadow had fallen over my life, and no matter how hard I tried to shake it off, it clung to me, whispering lies into my ear. "You don't belong here," it would say. "You're not important. You're just a shadow, an afterthought." And I believed it. I began to feel as though I was watching my life from a distance, disconnected from the joy and laughter around me. I felt trapped in a glass cage, peering out but never truly able to break free.

My siblings continued to thrive on noise and big, loud parties, while I sought refuge in the quiet, finding solace in the corners of rooms, always observing but never participating. I began to question everything, even my own worth. Why couldn't I just be like them? Why couldn't I enjoy life the way they did? The more I asked these questions, the more I spiraled into a pit of depression. It wasn't just sadness; it was a deep, consuming emptiness that swallowed me whole, making me wish I could disappear. The thought of ceasing to exist became strangely appealing. It felt like an escape from the relentless pressure of trying to make sense of a world that didn't seem to want me in it.

Growing up in a Christian household, God was always present, always part of the conversation. But as my inner struggles intensified, my relationship with God became fraught with questions and doubts. Why did He send me here? Why create me at all? Why wasn't I like my siblings? Why was I so emotional, so lost in my own head? I couldn't reconcile the idea of a loving God with the pain I was feeling. If God loved me, why did I feel so alone, so abandoned? These questions haunted me, filling me with a desperate need for answers. I begged God for something—anything that would help me make sense of it all, that would restore the hope I was rapidly losing. But the silence I received in return only deepened my despair.

And then, that voice from the beginning of my story returned. It whispered to me in the darkness, offering a way out. "You can end it all," it said, its tone soft, almost comforting. The idea began to take root in my mind, slowly but surely. Maybe this was the solution. Maybe if I ended it all, I would find peace, the kind of peace that had eluded me my whole life. It was tempting, so tempting, and I began to consider it seriously. I wanted to be okay, to have a smile on my face like my siblings always did. Could I escape my head and enjoy the crowd? Could I, too, just be a child and live life like everyone else? Or was I doomed to always be on the outside, looking in?

In those dark moments, I realized how desperately I craved connection and understanding, a longing to bridge the gap between my inner turmoil and the joyous existence I observed in others. I wanted to scream, to share my pain with someone who could truly hear me, to find solace in another soul who felt as lost as I did. But the fear of judgment kept me silent, wrapped in the suffocating blanket of loneliness. I remained a detective, still searching for answers, but now my cases were more urgent than ever. They were about survival, about finding a way to navigate this labyrinth of despair that had become my reality. I was desperate for a breakthrough, for a flicker of light in the dark, something to guide me back to a place where I felt alive, where I could finally belong

Psalm 139:13-16

You created every part of me; you put me together in my mother's womb. I will give thanks to you because I have been so amazingly and miraculously made. Your works are miraculous, and my soul is fully aware of this. My bones were not hidden from you when I was being made in secret, when I was being skillfully woven in an underground workshop. Your eyes saw me when I was only a fetus. Every day of my life was recorded in your book before one of them had taken place.

There are moments in life when we question our worth, when we feel disconnected, or as though we don't quite fit in. These feelings can stem from comparing ourselves to others, societal pressures, or moments of self-doubt. In those times, it's easy to forget that our worth is not determined by the opinions or expectations of others. Instead, we are reminded that we were crafted by God Himself— intentionally and with great care. We were formed with purpose, designed to reflect His love and creativity in a way that no one else can. It's empowering to remember that we are not accidents or random creations. From the very beginning, God saw us, knowing every part of us before we were even born.

Our uniqueness is a reflection of His divine design, and there is purpose woven into every aspect of our being. Even our imperfections and struggles serve a greater purpose in shaping who we are meant to be. We are fearfully and wonderfully made, a beautiful and intentional work of art. When the world makes us feel small, overlooked, or as though we're not enough, it's crucial to turn back to this truth: our value is not defined by external pressures or comparisons. Our worth comes from God alone, who created us with love and purpose.

The more we embrace this truth, the more we can confidently live as who we are, not as who the world tells us to be. It's only when we accept our identity in God that we find the courage to share our true selves with others and step into the place where we truly belong—surrounded by God's love and purpose for our lives.

Reflection questions:

1. Take a moment to reflect on areas where you feel the weight of comparison or the pressure to fit in. How do these influences affect how you see yourself? Do they make you question your worth or cause you to doubt who you truly are? How can you shift your focus from external approval to embracing the unique way God created you?

2. Consider what it means to be deeply known and loved by God. How might this truth change the way you handle the challenges and expectations that others place on you? How can leaning into God's love and purpose for your life help you stand firm in your identity, no matter what the world expects of you?

3. Reflect on moments when you've sought validation or tried to measure up to others' standards. In these moments, how can you remind yourself that your value is rooted not in people's opinions, but in the fact that God designed you with love and intention? What specific actions can you take to live out this truth in your daily life?

4. Think about the times when societal pressures or personal struggles have made you feel overwhelmed. How does knowing that Jesus has "overcome the world" influence your perspective on these challenges? What would it look like for you to lean into His victory over the world, rather than being defined by your circumstance?

I really want to hate you

I want to hate you so badly

Perhaps I do

Or maybe I hate myself

For being so weak

For not being able to fight back- I did fight back, you just happened to be stronger

I wasn't able to win the fight for my innocence

But then again Whether I had won or not is not the issue

My innocence was stolen the moment you came into my space and took what I didn't give you

What I thought was the most precious thing to me

Now I don't know anymore

I don't know how to feel safe

I don't know how to fully trust- I trusted you

I am not even attacking you at this point

I want to be innocent again

I want to feel safe again

I want to walk in the street without fear and without constantly looking over my shoulder.

IV.

I was always one of those kids who couldn't wait to get to school. Every day held the promise of adventure—whether it was seeing my teachers, playing with my friends, or running across the playground.

I memorized every song we were taught and threw myself into every school play. Growing up felt exciting, like each day opened up a world full of color, laughter, and possibility. Then, one day, someone befriended me.

I'd always been friendly, always eager to meet new people, so I welcomed it without hesitation. It was just one more reason to love school, or so I thought.

I remember how it started, even if the details have blurred over time. It was sometime after the fourth period, in the afternoon. I was on my way to the restroom, walking down the quiet hall, when I reached the restrooms, I felt a hand on my shoulder. I shrugged it off, thinking nothing of it. But then the touch changed, lingering, invasive. It wasn't right. I didn't know why, but a chill crept down my spine, and suddenly, I was afraid.

I froze.

Before I even understood what was happening, my skirt was gone. There was confusion—a deep, gut-wrenching sense that something was terribly wrong. I cried, but my voice seemed to dissolve in the empty restroom stalls.

And then she spoke, in a voice that frightened me, telling me not to tell anyone. I stood there, paralyzed, not fully grasping what had just happened but knowing, somehow, that I was trapped. If I told anyone, I was certain she'd hurt me again.

After that day, I couldn't bear the thought of going back to school. My parents didn't understand; I told them I was sick, and they believed me—they had no reason not to. I'd never lied before. They knew how much I loved school, so why would I make up excuses? Eventually, though, they convinced me to return. And when I did, it happened again.

And again.

Each time I went back, it was like stepping into a nightmare. I prayed to God—the God my father always spoke about, the one I'd been taught to trust. I begged Him to make it stop, to give me a way out. I pleaded with Him, telling Him I couldn't face another day. I was terrified, confused, and disgusted with myself, unable to reconcile how a place I once loved could become a prison.

Then, one day, right around the time when school was ending, we heard that the school was shutting down. I didn't have to go back. Relief washed over me, an almost tangible lightness replacing a weight I didn't realize I'd been carrying. For the first time in what felt like forever, I felt free—so free that I forgot to thank God for answering my prayer.

Thank you, Jesus.

The next year, I was sent to a new school. And there, things felt different. I made friends again, laughed again, and for a brief time, I was allowed to just be a kid. The nightmare faded, and I prayed

I'd never see that person again—not even in my dreams.

It was only much later that I began to realize the depth of what had happened to me. I wasn't raped, but I was sexually assaulted—by a woman. I can't remember exactly how much older she was, but I do know she was older than me, and that she seemed to know exactly what she was doing. I was too young to understand, but I would carry the impact of that violation with me for years.

She did things to my body that I cannot share, fearful of harming the fragile hearts of those who might hear. I remember feeling so utterly filthy— Oh Lord, I couldn't shake the feeling of dirtiness that clung to me after that experience.

I felt tainted, dirty, contaminated, and no amount of scrubbing or bathing seemed enough to wash it away. I would stand in the shower, using the harshest of soaps, but nothing could penetrate the layers of shame and self-loathing. No matter how hard I scrubbed, I still felt unclean.

I used to be a child who loved affection, someone who thrived on hugs and kisses, but after that, I wanted no part of it. I feared that a hug, a kiss, would lead to something dark and unwanted—something evil. I became ashamed of myself, ashamed of my own body. My body had become my enemy. If it were truly mine, how could it have attracted that predator? How could it betray me like this?

I lost my innocence long before I even understood what it meant. I kept asking myself, "What is wrong with me? Why do I have to be like this?"

Adding to the confusion was the fact that my first assailant was a woman. I convinced myself it wasn't such a big deal, that it wasn't worth causing a stir over. I told myself I should just forget about it and move on.

But my mind refused to let go of the memories. They twisted into nightmares, haunting me with her face. I would wake in the dead of night, my heart racing, always asking, "Why am I like this? Why can't I just forget?"

I wanted to run away, to escape, but no place felt safe. I was trapped inside my own mind, and that feeling lasted for years. As time passed, the image of her face faded from my memory, but her name remained, as if it has claimed a space in my mind without my permission. And now, all that's left is the memory of her name, and the birthmark that marred her face.

Ecclesiastes 4:1

I looked again and saw people being mistreated everywhere on earth. They were crying, but no one was there to offer comfort, and those who mistreated them were powerful.

Life can sometimes feel like a storm you can't outrun, with difficulties piling up and leaving you feeling small, unseen, or unheard. The world around you may seem indifferent, and the struggles you face can sometimes feel overwhelming—like you're carrying a weight that no one notices. Ecclesiastes captures this raw reality, painting a picture of a broken world where power often lies with the oppressor, and the oppressed are left in tears with no comforter. The repetition of this phrase underscores the deep hopelessness that can be felt in these moments of injustice and pain*.

Yet, as Christians, we know that this is not where the story ends. The brokenness of the world and the insufficiency of human solutions point us to the ultimate comfort found in Christ. He promises to be with us in our suffering, to heal our wounds, and to bring justice in His perfect time.

I remember vividly feeling stripped of power and comfort, left with the haunting memory of my oppressor and the weight of my own tears. It felt as if no one noticed, as if my cries for help vanished into the void. But even then, God saw it all. My tears never escaped His notice. He was there, present in my pain, whispering promises of healing and hope. Ecclesiastes reminds us that God's heart is not indifferent to our suffering. His eyes are always upon us, His heart forever with us.

When the powerful seem to hold all the answers and the world feels too heavy to bear, remember that God's comfort is far deeper than anything human strength can offer. His love is the gentle balm that heals wounds no one else sees. His presence is the steady hand that holds you up when you feel like you might fall. Christ's promise to be with us in our suffering doesn't remove the storms, but it assures us that we never face them alone.

This verse, though heavy with the weight of oppression, also carries the hope of redemption. It points us toward a God who not only sees our pain but has entered into it Himself through Jesus Christ. He knows the ache of our hearts in ways no one else can. And in His time, He will make all things right. Until then, He offers His presence as our comforter, His love as our strength, and His justice as our hope.

Reflection Questions:

1. Reflect on a time when you felt burdened by life's challenges, as if no one noticed your pain. How did that experience shape your view of yourself and others? In what ways can you draw comfort from knowing that God sees your tears and understands your heartache?

2. Think about situations where you've faced injustice or felt oppressed. How does the promise of God's ultimate justice and Christ's presence in suffering change how you view those experiences? How can this perspective help you find hope and peace?

3. Recall a time when you felt unseen or unheard. What would it look like to rest in the truth that your tears never escape God's notice? How might this shift your perspective on your current struggles?

4. How does recognizing the brokenness of the world help you depend more fully on God? What specific steps can you take to seek His comfort and rely on His justice rather than trying to fix everything on your own?

My mind is a mess

I feel trapped and entangled in my own emotions and perceptions, like a bird caught in a net of its own making. The way out is obvious; I can see the path to freedom just ahead. Yet, somehow, I can't seem to muster the strength or clarity to set myself free. How is it that I'm so ensnared by my own thoughts, unable to break free from the confines of my mind?

Every day, I wrestle with this internal struggle, questioning why I remain imprisoned by my own thinking. It feels as though I'm navigating a maze without an exit, each turn leading me back to the same place of confusion and frustration. If only I could unpack my mind, carefully sort through the tangled mess of emotions and perceptions and identify what exactly is refusing to make way for my freedom.

There must be something, some deep-seated

belief or fear, which holds me back. If I could pinpoint it, examine it, and understand its origins, perhaps I could remove it. Then, and only then, would I be able to release myself from these self-imposed chains and step into a state of true well-being.

Imagining that moment of liberation, I see myself finally able to enjoy my freedom, no longer weighed down by the invisible barriers I've constructed. The world would open up before me, full of possibilities and unburdened by the relentless cycle of self-doubt and entrapment. To reach that place, I must find the courage to delve deep into my psyche, to face whatever demons lie hidden, and to dismantle the walls that have kept me confined for so long.

Until then, the journey continues—a quest for self-awareness and inner peace, driven by the hope that one day, I will break free and fully embrace the freedom that awaits me.

V.

As everything around me began to change, I felt like life was racing forward while I stayed frozen in confusion. My older brother was preparing to leave for studies abroad, stepping into a life that seemed promising and full of potential. Meanwhile, my father grew more absorbed in his work, becoming a ghost at home, and my mother wrestled silently with demons no one else could see—demons that wore her down in ways I couldn't fully understand. In the midst of all this, I was coming of age, stepping into a world that had expectations for me, yet I had no idea who I was or what I wanted. Graduation loomed ahead, a symbol of freedom and possibility, but instead of excitement, I felt a deep sense of loss. I had studied literature and philosophy, hoping they'd offer me guidance, but instead, I felt empty, as if I'd been holding onto borrowed dreams.

I'd always loved fashion and dreamed of creating designs that would inspire others, maybe even rivaling icons like Karl Lagerfeld. Singing brought me joy, and I fantasized about sharing my voice with the world like Jennifer Hudson, exploring distant countries, and living a life marked by adventure. Yet, beneath all these dreams was a darker undercurrent—an unrelenting sense of self-doubt, accompanied by a whisper that I was inadequate, incapable, and directionless.

I vividly remember the moment I confronted this inner chaos.

In my culture, mental health isn't something we talk about; words like "depression" are as foreign as they are feared. Though technology was slowly bringing new ideas to our doorstep, I grew up in an environment where such thoughts were brushed aside, dismissed with a sidelong glance or a quick change of subject. This left me to wrestle alone, grappling with confusion and an endless sense of inadequacy. Books became my sanctuary. I devoured every story, seeking refuge between pages, where I could momentarily escape from my own life. I read obsessively, as if words alone could build a bridge to some peace within.

Then, one day, I saw my brother holding a book I'd never seen. My curiosity got the best of me, and I trailed him until he offered it to me without a word. The title was *Healing of Damaged Emotions* by David Seamands.*

I remember running to the living room, the weight of the book in my hands both comforting and daunting. As I read the first few lines, I felt something crack open within me, but I quickly closed the book, overwhelmed by the rawness of what it was revealing. A week passed before I found the courage to read it again, but this time, I wouldn't stop. Seamands' words seemed to mirror my soul, uncovering wounds I hadn't dared to look at. I came face-to-face with issues I hadn't even known had names: depression, low self-esteem, self-hatred, perfectionism, and so many others. Each label was like a revelation, peeling back layers of numbness that had kept me in darkness.

As I read, memories flooded back—days spent in bed, the weight of sadness pressing down like a heavy blanket, making it hard to breathe, the suffocating weight of despair that often enveloped me. I felt trapped in a fog, where every joyful moment was overshadowed by a nagging sense of inadequacy. I recalled moments when I stood in front of the mirror, dissecting every flaw, convinced that I could never be good enough. The relentless inner critic echoed in my mind, a voice that convinced me that happiness was an unattainable goal, a distant mirage.

With each page, I realized I had built a narrative in my mind that I was inherently "not good enough, that I needed to disappear." It was as though every part of me had been shaped by that single, destructive thought.

My relationship with my body was no exception. I was fixated on flaws no one else seemed to notice—the shape of my lips, the curve of my body, every detail scrutinized in the mirror until I felt like a stranger to myself. I hated my reflection, convinced I was flawed in ways others couldn't understand. My sisters, with their vibrant personalities, seemed effortlessly beautiful to me, a reminder of everything I thought I lacked. This daily ritual of comparison left me drained, always analyzing, always certain that I fell short.

Why was it that I saw beauty in everyone but myself?

I'd perfected the art of presenting my face to the world—an outer mask I clung to, as if it were all I had to offer. I was fixated on how others saw me, searching their eyes for approval, without ever considering that what I saw might be my own reflection, a projection of all the insecurities I'd carried for so long.

I found myself measuring against the beauty I saw in others, as if they'd succeeded where I'd failed, as if they possessed something elusive, something I'd never have. But maybe, just maybe, it was not that I was lacking. Maybe it's that I'd never taken the time to look beyond my own doubts. It was easier to see flaws in myself when I'd never sat still, never letting myself be quiet enough to hear the whisper of my own worth.

I'd grown used to pointing out all the ways I fell short, focusing on the parts of me I wished I could change. I hadn't realized that the beauty I sought in others could be inside me too—hidden beneath the noise of my own harsh judgments. What if I paused long enough to find it? To sit with myself as I am, to see beyond the surface I've been hiding behind. Perhaps I would realize that the beauty I've been searching for wasn't missing; it was maybe simply waiting for me to notice it.

Compliments felt like lies. I couldn't accept them, couldn't see in myself the worth others seemed to see. Instead, I was trapped in a loop of mistakes and missed chances, where every error echoed that familiar inner voice telling me I was a failure. I struggled to understand why God had made me this way—why He had allowed me to feel so painfully out of place in my own skin.

I questioned Him often, in moments of raw honesty, asking why I was burdened with such deep self-loathing. I would tell Him that I hated the person He had created, that I despised the way I looked and felt, unable to reconcile His love with the person I saw in the mirror. It was a dark, relentless spiral, one that left me feeling isolated, even from God. And though I cried out for change, it felt like my pleas echoed back, unanswered, as I continued to battle this inner torment that seemed endless and inescapable. This was the depth of my struggle—the daily, unspoken war that went on in silence, hidden behind a smile. It was a war I was barely surviving, each day bringing new scars that no one else could see.

I was on the chubbier side compared to my sisters, and I began to believe that if I could make myself thinner, I could be as beautiful as they were. I remember when we would go shopping for clothes. It was always so rare for us to find something that would fit me right, while my sisters seemed to have no trouble picking out clothes that looked great on them. They would come home with bags full of new outfits, while I stayed behind, feeling bad about the way I looked. So my solution to this issue was to starve myself.

I thought that if I just didn't eat, I could shrink into the version of myself I imagined would be beautiful—the version of myself that would finally be worthy of the world's approval. I was obsessed with the idea that the thinner I became, the more I could match up to my sisters and to the beauty I saw in others. It was an attempt to erase what I thought were my imperfections, to mold myself into something I could feel proud of.

But instead of gaining the beauty and confidence I so desperately wanted, I found myself sinking deeper into a spiral of self-hate. The more I starved myself, the more I lost touch with who I was. My body became something I didn't recognize, and the emptiness inside me only grew. My obsession with my appearance became a prison, one that took me further and further from the person I could have been.

But somewhere, buried deep beneath all the self-doubt and despair, a part of me still clung to the belief that there was something more waiting—something beyond the mirror, beyond the noise of my inner critic. The path to healing seemed impossible, yet the thought of it—however faint—was enough to keep me moving forward, step by fragile step.

I didn't know what it would take, or how long it would take, but I was starting to realize that the journey ahead was less about changing what I saw in the mirror, and more about learning to see myself differently—without the filters of fear and shame.

And so, I began.

Psalm 34:10

The LORD is near to those who are discouraged; he saves those who have lost all hope.* The LORD is close to the brokenhearted, and he delivers those whose spirit has been crushed.*

In my own journey, there were moments when the weight of self-doubt and insecurity felt unbearable. I convinced myself that I was too broken, too flawed, or too unworthy to be healed. The pain felt isolating, as though no one, not even God, could understand the depth of my struggles. But as I reflected on Psalm 34:18, I began to see things differently. This verse reminded me of a profound truth: God does not distance Himself from our pain; He draws near. He is close to those who are brokenhearted, offering His comfort and healing to spirits that feel crushed under the weight of life's burdens.

In those moments of despair, I started to

understand something transformative. My worth was not defined by my flaws, my failures, or the harsh judgments I often placed on myself. Instead, it was rooted in how deeply God loves me—even in my brokenness. His love is not conditional on my ability to "fix" myself or be perfect. It is steadfast, unchanging, and present in the very moments I felt the most unworthy of it.

God's presence doesn't promise an immediate end to the struggle or a quick solution to the pain. But it offers something far greater: the assurance that we are never truly alone. In the midst of my darkest seasons, when I felt overwhelmed by feelings of inadequacy, God's closeness became my anchor. His love whispered to my heart that no wound was too deep for His healing, no burden too heavy for Him to carry alongside me.

If you, too, are battling feelings of self-loathing, inadequacy, or brokenness, know this: God sees you exactly as you are and does not turn away.

He desires to heal the wounds you think are too deep, to replace your despair with His hope, and to walk with you through the darkness into the light of His healing. You don't need to have it all together to come to Him. In fact, He welcomes you, especially in your brokenness, because His strength is made perfect in our weakness. God's nearness is not just a comforting thought; it is a life-changing truth. His grace meets us right where we are, assuring us that we are never alone and always loved. You can trust Him to be your refuge, your healer, and the One who saves your crushed spirit and brings you into the fullness of His love.

Reflection Questions:

1. Think about the emotional battles you've faced. What has been weighing heavily on your heart? What would it look like to invite God into that pain and let Him begin to heal it?

2. Consider the way you view yourself. How might your perception of your own worth change if you accepted God's view of you, rather than relying on your own inner critic?

3. In moments of struggle, how can you remind yourself of God's presence and His desire to heal you? Reflect on practical ways you can invite peace and hope into your day-to-day life,

such as through prayer, journaling, or meditating on verses like Psalm 34:18

4. Healing doesn't always happen instantly, but it begins when we open our hearts to God's love. What is one small step you can take today to draw closer to Him in your journey of healing?

Innocent again

I want to be innocent again.

Free from self-doubt, From self-hatred that eats away at my soul,

From pride that blinds me, and from the fear that paralyzes me.

Release me from the grip of those terrible memories—

Though I've forgiven and been forgiven, they still linger, haunting me in the quiet moments.

Lift the heavy burden of guilt I've carried for what I was powerless to prevent,

And even for the choices I made when I could have done better but didn't.

I am desperate to be clean again, For You, for myself, and for those I love.

I long to shed the weight of my past, to be free of its hold on me.

If I could be new again…

Please, strip away the layers of pride that have built up over time, Until I am humble, like Jesus, who did not see equality with God as something to be grasped but emptied Himself in love.

Free me, forgive me, for all the pain I've caused others and myself.

Let Your love wash over me and cleanse me once more,

So that I may stand before You, renewed and whole.

VI.

When I first arrived in the U.S., everything felt foreign—new language, unfamiliar faces, a culture that seemed to swallow me whole. I was accompanied only by my brother, and Temple University became my gateway into this strange new world. As I studied English, I found myself longing for a sense of belonging, something that echoed the familiarity of home.

One day, I stumbled upon a group of girls who introduced themselves as members of ENC, a Christian organization. I didn't know what ENC stood for, but I immediately recognized the faith they shared. Growing up in a Christian household, I felt drawn to them, hoping to find a piece of comfort amidst the disorientation of my new surroundings. Despite our different backgrounds, our common faith was enough to forge a connection.

What truly struck me was the diversity of the group. They came from various backgrounds, spoke different languages, and their skin tones were as varied as the places they hailed from. I had never witnessed anything like it—individuals from such different walks of life gathered together in unity, all bound by one thing: Jesus. So, they invited me to one of their gatherings and I went gladly.

That day, they spoke passionately about the grace of God, and for some reason, their words resonated with me in a way they never had before. They shared about our shared humanity, how we all fall short, and how God sent His Son to reconcile us to Him. Their insights about unmerited grace felt like a light breaking through the fog of my confusion, igniting a realization within me. I didn't even realize how desperately I needed to hear that message until that moment.

After that day, I eagerly sought to immerse myself further in the group. I formed friendships that still enrich my life today, and I believed that joining ENC was about building community. But little did I know, God was preparing my heart for something much more profound—something I wasn't yet ready to confront.

Forgiveness.

That word began to echo in my mind, persistent and unavoidable, like a haunting melody I couldn't silence. At first, I didn't understand why it kept surfacing. I was wrestling with the reality that God was calling me to forgive the person who had assaulted me, a thought I wanted to push away at all costs. I resisted confronting this painful chapter of my life, afraid of the turmoil it would stir within me. But eventually, after much internal struggle, I reached out to one of the campus ministers, Will—a kind man whose compassion I found comforting—and shared my dilemma with him. How does one forgive someone who has caused a deep, lasting pain?

Will's response was simple yet profound. He reminded me that forgiveness is a gift God gives us, saying, "We sin against God every day, yet He forgives us. How can we expect to be forgiven if we aren't willing to forgive others?" His words struck a chord, but they also opened a floodgate of resistance within me.

I struggled immensely with the concept of forgiveness, as my understanding was painfully limited. I believed that forgiving her would mean she would escaped unpunished, free to continue with her life while I remained shackled by my trauma. My anger and resentment felt like a form of justice—punishment for her actions that I believed she deserved.

I couldn't shake the conviction that letting go of my anger would diminish the severity of what she had done. It felt as if I would be forced to brush aside the feelings of dirtiness and anguish, the nightmares that haunted me, and simply move on. She didn't just take something from me; she robbed me of my innocence, my sense of safety, and my childhood. How could I ever extend forgiveness to someone who had inflicted such harm? What right did she have to my grace?

I found myself wishing for her to suffer, to feel the weight of her actions, to be punished in some way—anything but simply letting it go. "whoever they are, bring them to God and ask Him to help you forgive them," Will suggested, but I had never dared to voice the depths of my pain; no one knew the full extent of what I had endured.

Will knew only that I was struggling with unforgiveness, and I convinced myself that if he truly understood my experience, maybe he would respond differently; maybe he wouldn't view it as a matter of just handing it over to God. It felt like an oversimplification of something profoundly complex and painful. The idea of forgiving and doing nothing felt suffocating; it seemed too kind, too generous for someone who had hurt me so deeply.

I am kind of curious now, I wonder what he would have said if I had shared the whole story. I believe he would have said the same thing; for what it is worth I am grateful he was the person I talked to.

I smiled and thanked Will, but inside, I felt a storm of conflict. His words lingered in my mind, haunting me, challenging me in ways I wasn't ready to confront. Deep down, I knew I had to face this, but I wasn't prepared. Not today, not tomorrow. Perhaps not ever. If God wanted me to forgive, He would have to orchestrate that change within me, because my heart was far from ready to take that monumental step.

Matthew 18:21-35

Then Peter came to Jesus and asked, "Lord, if my brother keeps on sinning against me, how many times do I have to forgive him? Seven times?" No, not seven times," answered Jesus, "but seventy times seven, because the Kingdom of heaven is like this.

Once there was a king who decided to check on his servants' accounts. He had just begun to do so when one of them was brought in who owed him millions of dollars. The servant did not have enough to pay his debt, so the king ordered him to be sold as a slave, with his wife and his children and all that he had, in order to pay the debt. The servant fell on his knees before the king. 'Be patient with me,' he begged, 'and I will pay you everything!' The king felt sorry for him, so he forgave him the debt and let him go.

Then the man went out and met one of his fellow servants who owed him a few dollars. He *grabbed him and started choking him. 'Pay back what you owe me!' he said. His fellow servant fell down and begged him, 'Be patient with me, and I will pay you back!' But he refused; instead, he had him thrown into jail until he should pay the debt.*

When the other servants saw what had happened, they were very upset and went to the king and told him everything. So he called the servant in. 'You worthless slave!' he said. 'I forgave you the whole amount you owed me, just because you asked me to.

You should have had mercy on your fellow servant, just as I had mercy on you. The king was very angry, and he sent the servant to jail to be punished until he should pay back the whole amount. And Jesus concluded, That is how my Father in heaven will treat every one of you unless you forgive your brother from your heart.

In this passage, Jesus teaches a profound lesson on forgiveness, one that challenges us to move beyond human limitations and reflect the boundless mercy of God. Peter, trying to grasp the limits of forgiveness, asks if forgiving someone seven times would be enough. Jesus answers by expanding Peter's understanding, saying, "seventy times seven." This wasn't about literal math but about the boundless nature of forgiveness that should characterize those who follow Christ.

To drive the lesson home, Jesus tells the parable of a servant who owed an unthinkable debt to a king. When the servant pleaded for mercy, the king forgave the entire debt—a gift of grace beyond comprehension. Yet, that same servant turned around and refused to forgive a fellow servant who owed him a far smaller debt. Instead of showing the mercy he had received, he demanded repayment, revealing a heart unchanged by the forgiveness he had been given.

This parable paints a vivid picture of the forgiveness we receive from God. Our sins create a debt we could never repay, yet through Jesus, God forgives us completely. It's a forgiveness so deep, so transformative, that it calls us to respond by forgiving others in the same way. But forgiveness is not always easy. It requires humility, compassion, and a willingness to let go of resentment. It means choosing to release the offense, not because the person deserves it, but because we have been forgiven much.

If you're struggling to forgive, remember the grace God has shown you. His forgiveness is limitless, not based on our worthiness, but on His great love. When we reflect on the magnitude of His mercy, we're empowered to extend that same forgiveness to others, freeing not only them but also ourselves from the chains of bitterness. Forgiveness is not just an act of obedience; it's a gift that transforms hearts—ours and theirs.

Refection questions

1. Consider the magnitude of the debt forgiven in the parable. Do you find yourself keeping a "limit" on how much you're willing to forgive someone? How does Jesus' teaching of "seventy times seven" challenge that mindset? How does this help you understand the depth of God's forgiveness toward you? How can reflecting on this truth empower you to forgive others?

2. Think about a person or situation where you're struggling to extend forgiveness. What might it look like to forgive them "from the heart," as Jesus teaches? What practical steps can you take to begin that process?

3. How does the servant's refusal to forgive a smaller debt after being forgiven a much larger one challenge you? In what ways do you struggle with letting go of past hurts, and how does the parable of the unforgiving servant confront those struggles? In what ways can you ensure that God's forgiveness of you transforms your attitude toward others?

4. Forgiveness doesn't mean forgetting the offense or dismissing its impact. How can you balance acknowledging the hurt while choosing to release the resentment and trust God with justice?

Dear God

Please keep me from sinning against you

Oh, help me to never be controlled by sin. I pray that sin never has such a hold on me to the point of killing my conscience

Don't allow my sin to creep in and make me forget that I love your law and my most earnest desire is to obey you and live a life that honors you

Speak to me through your spirit and if I fail to listen, send people my way, your people to bring me back to the right path. And even if that fails too

Father make my heart malleable in your hand so that your voice and your love will break all the walls surrounding my heart.

Take my pride away and show me the world in your hand, remind me that you are God, above all and everything. Please free me from my pride. In Jesus name I pray, Amen

VII.

I used to believe that I wasn't a sinner, that my actions were blameless. For a long time, I believed I wasn't a sinner in my daily life. I thought as long as I avoided big sins, I was fine. I knew humans are inherently sinful, but I didn't recognize the smaller sins I was committing—whether in my thoughts, words, or actions. I didn't see how even the little things could still be sins. I saw no need for forgiveness, so why should I extend it to her or anyone at all?

At the same time, the shame of my experience kept me silent, reinforcing my belief that I was justified in my anger and resentment. I told myself that my pain was proof of her wrongdoing, and the thought of forgiving her felt like I would be diminishing my own suffering. The burden of resentment became a way to hold her accountable, even if it was only in my heart.

Pride clouded my judgment, leading me to believe I was justified in my feelings- perhaps in some way I was-. I deceived myself into thinking I was in the right, unaware of the depths of my own heart. I made a commitment: anytime the word "forgive" crossed my mind, I would fight back, recounting all that had been done to me, the pain I endured, as if somehow that would convince God to take my side. That was very exhausting.

One day, as I read my Bible, I stumbled upon the parable of the servant who was thrown into prison for not forgiving his brother's debt (See Matthew 18:23-35). Suddenly, the weight of those verses hit me. It became clear that my righteousness didn't stem from my actions but from the sacrifice of Jesus. I realized that I wasn't blameless; I was a sinner. To me, sinning had always meant the big offenses—murder, theft, those dramatic acts. I didn't recognize the sin of resentment, the bitterness in my heart when God said vengeance belonged to Him, or the pride that blinded me to my own faults. I ignored the rebellion and idolatry lurking in my heart.

My ignorance had made me think I was blameless, leading me to believe I didn't need forgiveness.

Overwhelmed, I fell to my knees, crying out to God, begging for His forgiveness, asking Him to rid me of my pride and help me recognize my sins so I could repent and restore my relationship with Him. I realized I was a sinner—constantly in need of God's grace. That day, I came to understand my need for Jesus.

And then, in my heart, I heard Him say, "give her to me." I knew He was referring to the girl who had hurt me. I couldn't. I fought back tears, feeling the struggle within me, but God wasn't angry; He was gentle and understanding. He continued to urge me to give her to Him. The more He spoke, the more peace I felt about letting her go. It was hard because I didn't know how God would handle her, and a part of me didn't want Him to forgive her as fully as He had just forgiven me.

But I was tired of holding on to the anger, so I finally released her. I surrendered her to God that day. In that moment, I experienced a profound peace, as if a heavy weight had been lifted off my shoulders. For the first time, I felt free, knowing that I had taken a step toward true forgiveness, trusting God to handle the situation as only He could.

A Little Extra:

I don't remember exactly how much time had passed after that encounter with God. I went to a church near my house, seeking a sense of normalcy. That Sunday after the service, I found myself sitting at the front, alone. I wasn't sure why I couldn't get up. Maybe it was exhaustion, maybe it was something deeper that I hadn't yet processed. I sat there, almost frozen in place, when suddenly, without warning, I felt this rush of emotion rise up from somewhere deep inside me. It was as if a dam had broken, and I didn't know how to stop it. Before I realized what was happening, tears started pouring out. But these weren't the delicate, silent tears you can wipe away with a tissue. No, these were the deep, gut-wrenching sobs—the kind that made it feel like every part of me was coming undone. I cried like a baby in pain, the sound of it filling the room. It wasn't pretty, but I couldn't help it.

I don't remember exactly who came to check on me first—whether it was the pastor or his wife—but I remember someone approaching. They gently asked what was going on, and though I don't recall their exact words, something in their presence made me feel safe. I began to speak, my voice shaky, barely above a whisper. For the first time ever, I opened up about the assault. I didn't go into all the details, but I shared enough to release something that had been buried deep inside me for years. The words seemed to spill out of me without my permission. It was shocking, even to me. I had never planned to talk about it, especially not there, not like that. It just happened, as if the weight of it could no longer be contained.

The pastor's wife listened, her eyes full of compassion. She didn't rush me, didn't push for more than I was ready to share. And before I knew it, there was another lady by my side. Then, the pastor joined us, and suddenly, they were all praying over me. I closed my eyes, letting the words of their prayers wash over me like a gentle wave. They prayed for what felt like a long time, and I remember vividly when they began praying the blood of Jesus over me.

I had always known about the power of the blood of Jesus to cleanse us from sin—that was something I'd heard growing up, something I believed in. But in that moment, I experienced something entirely new. As they prayed, I felt an overwhelming sense of cleanliness, not just in my spirit but in my body. It was as if the dirtiness I had carried since the assault—the filth I could never scrub away, no matter how hard I tried— was being lifted off of me.

That day, something shifted. After that prayer, I felt a purity, a freshness, that I had never felt before. It was as if every layer of filth, every ounce of shame, was stripped away in an instant. I thought I was dreaming. I sat there for a moment, trying to process it. How could something so simple, so spiritual, have such a profound effect on me physically? I had no words for it. I could only feel the lightness, the freedom.

I don't think I will ever forget that feeling. I smiled all the way home, grinning like a child. My brother glanced at me from the driver's seat, probably wondering what had gotten into me, but he didn't say a word. He just drove, and I sat there, reveling in this newfound peace. When we got home, I did something I hadn't done in a long time—I challenged myself. Normally, I would have rushed to the bathroom to take a second, third, or even fourth shower of the day, desperate to feel clean. But that day, I didn't. I decided to stick with the one shower I had taken that morning. I told myself, "Let's see what happens. Let's see if that overwhelming urge to wash myself will come back."

But it didn't.

I went to bed that night, still feeling clean, still feeling free. I lay down, expecting the usual discomfort, the sense that my skin was crawling, begging to be scrubbed away. But nothing. No filth, no shame. Just peace. I slept like a baby that night, the best sleep I'd had in years. I woke up the next morning, and to my surprise, I still felt clean and for the first time in forever, her face did not haunt my dreams. It was as if the years of feeling dirty, the compulsion to wash, and the constant waking up in the middle of the night had vanished overnight.

How long had it been since the assault? Ten years? Maybe more. But from that day forward, I never felt dirty again. Not once. Even now, as I reflect on it, I still can't fully explain it, except to say that the blood of Jesus is powerful. More powerful than I had ever imagined.

That day, God didn't just heal me—He set me free. Free from shame, free from the pain, free from the burden I had carried for so long. And I will never forget it. That transformative moment in church marked the beginning of a new chapter in my life, one I hadn't anticipated. After prayer, I felt an overwhelming sense of relief, as if a heavy weight had been lifted off my shoulders. For the first time in years, I was not just free from the feeling of dirtiness, but also from the invisible chains of shame and regret that had held me captive. The blood of Jesus had not only cleansed my body; it had renewed my spirit; it had set me free to walk in the light of God's grace.

As I reflect on that day in church, I am forever grateful for the divine intervention that led me to that moment of prayer. It was not just an isolated event but the catalyst for a life transformed. I stand as a testament to the healing power of God—a power that can restore, redeem, and renew. This journey of healing was not linear. There were days when the shadows of my past crept back in, moments when I felt the urge to retreat into old patterns of shame and isolation. But now, armed with the truth of my experience and the power of prayer, I was able to fight back. I learned to bring my struggles into the light, to share them with trusted friends and mentors who could support me in my walk.

I john 1:7-9

But if we really walk in the Light that is, live each and every day in the fellowship of Christ, as He Himself is in the Light, we have true, unbroken fellowship with one another, and the blood of Jesus His Son cleanses us from all sin by erasing the stain of sin. If we say we have no sin, we are deceiving ourselves and the truth is not in us. If we freely admit that we have sinned and confess our sins, He is faithful and just to forgive us our sins and to cleanse us continually from all unrighteousness—He is truly our way of salvation.

Forgiveness is one of the most powerful gifts God has given us. Not only have we received forgiveness from God, but we are also called to extend that same forgiveness to others. The grace we've been shown through Christ's sacrifice compels us to release others from the weight of their wrongdoings, just as God has released us from our own offenses.

As **1 John 1:7-9** reminds us: We are cleansed from all sin through the blood of Jesus, not because we deserve it, but because of His redemptive work on the cross. In the same way, we must forgive, not because others have earned it, but because Christ's grace compels us to extend that same mercy.

The blood of Jesus is the basis of our forgiveness. His blood cleanses us from all sin, removing the stain of guilt and shame that once held us captive. The power of His blood not only offers forgiveness but also transforms us, making us new. It is through the blood of Jesus that we are freed from the chains of sin and filth, washed clean and made whole again.

Sometimes, our healing is intricately tied to our ability to forgive. Holding onto bitterness, anger, or resentment can create a spiritual block that prevents us from experiencing the fullness of God's peace and healing. When we forgive, we free ourselves from the emotional chains that bind us.

It's not about excusing or justifying the actions of others; it's about releasing the control that hurt, and offenses have over us. By forgiving, we open ourselves up to God's healing, which flows more freely when we choose to walk in His grace toward others. The power of the blood of Jesus is a constant reminder that forgiveness is possible, that no sin is too great to be washed away, and that through Him, we are made new.

In the same way we've been forgiven, we must forgive. We must also remember that forgiveness is not just a choice—it's a powerful act of obedience that aligns our hearts with God's heart. It is through forgiveness that we not only experience personal freedom but also reflect God's love and mercy to the world around us. Through Christ, we are cleansed, healed, and restored—free to walk in the fullness of His grace.

Reflection questions:

1. How does forgiving others — especially when they don't deserve it — reveal the depth of your obedience to God and reflect His heart of mercy to the world around you? What would happen if you stopped waiting for others to earn your forgiveness, and instead chose to extend it freely, as God does for you?

2. Reflecting on the cleansing power of Jesus' blood, how do you view your past sins and mistakes now? What would happen if you allowed the full weight of His sacrifice to wash away every stain, every shame, and every memory of guilt you've been holding onto?

3. Can you pinpoint the emotional walls you've built up as a result of hurt or betrayal? How might releasing those

wounds through forgiveness unlock the flow of God's healing in your life, transforming your ability to love and be loved?

4. When you consider forgiveness not as excusing wrongs, but as a powerful choice to release the hold of bitterness and resentment, how might this perspective shift your approach to both the people who've hurt you and your own healing process?

Searching in vain

Sometimes it feels like I'm searching for something, but I can't quite grasp what it is. My heart craves something I cannot identify, and each moment leaves me longing. I try different things, but none of them seem to satisfy. There's always a part of me that remains untouched, no matter what I do. Even if something manages to reach that hidden part, the satisfaction is fleeting. I'm always left wanting more. What am I looking for? What is this elusive thing that I'm so desperately searching for?

It feels like my heart is thirsty, but for what? It's strange that I can't even answer that question. I can't identify what it is that my heart desires so deeply. I make decisions and try new things, but I can never stick with them for long. The more I try, the more it feels like I'm not doing the right thing. And when I stop, I feel guilty, as if I'm not doing enough. What is it?

I remember a phrase one of my professors said back in school: "There is a void inside every human being that has the shape of God. No matter what they try to fill their hearts with, it will never be filled because it needs God." Is that what I'm experiencing right now? Am I searching for God at the wrong places?

VIII.

One thing I had always grappled with was a profound sense of loneliness and a deep feeling of emptiness. It wasn't just fleeting emotions but ever-present shadows that followed me. Even in the midst of my siblings, I never felt like I belonged. They seemed to have their own rhythm, their own connection, and I was always on the outside, looking in. High school didn't help. My friends were quick to point out my flaws—most of which I was already painfully aware of. Their casual remarks chipped away at whatever confidence I had left, feeding my insecurities like fuel to a fire.

In my desperation to be accepted, I thought maybe if I just created a different version of myself, a new image, I could finally fit in. I wore a mask, carefully crafted stories to make me seem more interesting, more likable, more... everything. My friends took notice; they learned in, eager to hear my stories, drawn to this persona I had created. But despite all my efforts, the loneliness persisted, gnawing at me.

I was the odd one out, always out of sync, always apart from the world around me. No matter what I did, it was never enough.

So, I began to think, maybe if I had a romantic relationship, someone who saw only me, who cherished me, maybe then I wouldn't feel so alone. I prayed fervently, "God, send me someone." I imagined that if I found that person, we would get married, have children, and not only would my heart finally feel full, but my life, my home, would be overflowing with love.

But time passed, and nothing changed. I waited, and with each passing day, the weight of my loneliness grew heavier. Depression began to creep in, slowly but surely, casting everything in a gray, hopeless light. Why did my life have to be like this? Why couldn't I be like everyone else, whole, and happy?

Then, one day, a friend invited me to a birthday party. I didn't expect much, just another event to get through. But there he was—a boy who gave me attention, spoke to me as if I had mattered. We agreed to go out on a date, and soon enough, we were in a relationship.

For the first time, I thought, "This is it. I won't be alone anymore. I've finally found my person." The thrill of it all kept me occupied, and for a while, I believed that the void inside me would be filled. But as the newness of the relationship wore off, I realized something disturbing—I still felt alone. He had his own life, separate from me, and even when we were together, I couldn't shake the emptiness inside. What was wrong with me? Why did my heart still feel so hollow, so void of connection? Being in a relationship hadn't cured my loneliness as I'd hoped. I convinced myself that maybe marriage was the missing piece. "Be patient," I told myself, "Once we get married, things will be different. It will get better."

The more I thought about marrying him, the less I believed it would fill the emptiness I felt inside, but I was desperate for it to. I didn't just love him—I was crazy about the man. I wanted him to be my world, my everything, the center of my universe. I imagined a life where our identities were so merged that no one could tell where he ended, and I began. I molded my life around his desires, worshipping his every word as if it were gospel. Pleasing him became my purpose, and the thought of disappointing him terrified me. When I inevitably fell short, I only doubled my efforts—pouring more love, more energy into trying to meet his expectations. I believed that if I could just perfect myself in his eyes, he could fill the void inside me. I was convinced that if I could be everything he wanted, I would no longer feel the crushing loneliness and emptiness within.

But I had come to the painful realization that I had been idolizing my relationship. I had placed it on such a high pedestal that even life itself, even God, couldn't compete. My partner's happiness became my happiness; he was my everything. I was so focused on trying to mold him into something that would fill that void within me that I couldn't see the cracks in our relationship. I valued him so much that I truly believed I couldn't survive in this world without him. He became my purpose, my standard. In my mind, he was it—mine forever. I didn't dare wish for anyone else.

Not because he was perfect, but because I wanted to be like my mom. She only ever loved my dad, through it all, until death finally did part them. I wanted that so badly for myself that I refused to acknowledge anything that hinted at something being wrong in my relationship. I had made a commitment in my heart to follow her example, even when it meant turning a blind eye to the obvious. It had taken me so long to fall in love in the first place, to allow someone not just close to me, but into my heart. For years, I didn't trust people; I didn't let anyone know me or get close enough to hurt me. But with him, I let him in. I gave him a place in my heart that should have belonged to God alone.

He became my world, and I was so consumed by the idea of love that I didn't see how much I had pushed God aside. I had unknowingly placed my relationship on the throne of my heart, challenging

God's rightful place, and arousing His jealousy—
and oh, how serious that was.

I was terrified that I'd never love again. After all, it
had taken so long for it to happen in the first
place—maybe that was a sign that this relationship
was meant to be. I feared that if I let go, I'd never
find someone else. What if this was my only
chance? I was afraid that, if I let go of this
relationship, I might end up being trapped in a
loveless relationship, clinging to the hope that it
would someday come to life and grow, and that
was too much for me to bear. I couldn't face that
reality, so I held on with everything in me, hoping
my faith would keep us together.

But I was blind to the truth: one cannot arouse
God's jealousy and walk away unscathed. His
jealousy isn't like ours; it's pure, righteous, and
protective. There is always a reckoning for those
who put someone else in His place. "I am a jealous
God," He said, over and over, but I ignored the
warnings, too blinded by my own desires to realize
the cost of my ignorance. I didn't see that I had

been holding on to something that was slipping away from me, something that was never meant to take the place of God in my heart.

Psalm 42

As a deer gets thirsty for streams of water, I truly am thirsty for you, my God.
In my heart, I am thirsty for you, the living God.
When will I see your face? Day and night my tears are my only food, as everyone keeps asking,
"Where is your God?"
Sorrow floods my heart, when I remember leading the worshipers to your house. I can still hear them shout their joyful praises.
Why am I discouraged? Why am I restless? I should trust you, LORD.
I will praise you again because you help me, and you are my God.
I am deeply discouraged, and so I think about you here where the Jordan begins at Mount Hermon and at Mount Mizar.
Your vicious waves have swept over me like an angry ocean or a roaring waterfall.

Every day, you are kind, and at night you give me a song as my prayer to you, the God of my life. You are my mighty rock.
Why have you forgotten me? Why must enemies mistreat me and make me sad? Even my bones are in pain, while all day long my enemies sneer and ask,
"Where is your God?"
Why am I discouraged?
Why am I restless?
I trust you, LORD! And I will praise you again because you help me, and you are my God.

As I navigated through a season of deep emptiness, I realized something crucial: no human could ever fill the void I carried inside. I had been looking to others for validation, for healing, but I was always left thirsty, longing for something that could never fully satisfy. It was like trying to drink from a cup that would never be full. Psalm 42 captures this feeling perfectly when it says, *"As the deer pants for the water brooks, so my soul pants for You, O God. My soul thirsts for God, for the living God. When shall I come and appear before God?"*. My soul was desperate for something real, something life-giving, but I didn't know what. I was thirsty for more, but the things I thought would fill me left me parched and searching.

I had sought love and acceptance from people, thinking that if I could just find the right relationship, the right affirmation, everything would fall into place. But no matter how much I tried, I always ended up feeling more empty. It wasn't until I began to let go of that search for external validation that I realized: only Jesus, the living water, could quench that thirst. His presence, His love, fills every empty space in us. When I finally stopped looking to others and turned to Him, I discovered that He is enough—more than enough to fill the places in me I thought were beyond repair.

I used to believe that I needed to fix myself first before I could really experience His love, but that's not how it works. I had to let go of the idea that I had to be "whole" before I could be loved. Jesus is the one who fills in all the cracks we try so hard to hide. Just like the psalmist says, *"Why are you in despair, O my soul? And why have you become disturbed within me? Hope in God, for I shall again praise Him, the help of my countenance and my God"*, I realized that my hope could no longer be in anything or anyone else. It had to rest in God alone. It's in that place of surrender, when I stopped trying to fill my own empty spaces, that I found peace in the most unexpected way.

What I had longed for in relationships, in accomplishments, or in things, was never going to give me the peace I sought. Only Jesus' love, that deep, unconditional love, can satisfy every longing. In Him, there is no lack, no emptiness. His grace fills the broken places I've tried to cover up for so long. He meets us right where we are—not when we're perfect, but in the middle of our thirst. And in that moment, we can feel the peace that only He can provide. It's a peace that says, "You are enough, and I am enough for you."

Reflection Questions:

1. When you look at the things you've sought to fill the emptiness within you, how do you feel knowing that each of them ultimately left you thirsting for more? What does this reveal about the nature of your longing, and how might it be pointing you to something deeper than what you've been searching for?

2. In what ways has your hope been placed in things or people who inevitably fail to live up to your expectations? How does it feel to accept that true hope—hope that cannot be shaken—is found only in God alone, and how might this change how you face challenges or desires?

3. How do you reconcile the truth that Jesus' love is enough to satisfy every longing within you, even the parts of you that feel most broken or incomplete? How might embracing His sufficiency bring a peace that no person, accomplishment, or thing could ever offer?

4. If you truly grasped the idea that you no longer need to search for fulfillment outside of God, how would this change the way you approach your desires and relationships? What might it look like to stop striving and instead choose to rest in the fullness of His grace?

My funny valentine

In a world filled with harsh people and tough circumstances that break us, it's crucial to be each other's safe place, the one we can run to for comfort and strength. We encounter people who love and others who betray us. Amidst this pitiless world, I need to know that you've got my back and that you won't turn against me.

Whenever you don't accept me for who I am, it breaks me. Yes, I am fragile, and my feelings get hurt, but it's only with you that I am this vulnerable. I know you are tough and want me to be tough too, but the world and its people are already toughening me up.

I don't want to turn to you and see the world. I don't want to seek comfort only to find spikes instead. I don't want to seek being cherished and find painful words that leave me shattered and unable to move forward. Aren't you my lover, the one who loves every part of me?

Someone who understands that my weaknesses make me even more beautiful because they allow me to recognize yours too.

We are imperfect people seeking perfect love that we can never find in each other, but only in the one who made us. I know you can never love me perfectly because I am imperfect and so are you.

IX.

You've probably guessed it: that relationship didn't last. It wasn't long before we began to drift apart. Work took us to different states, and soon enough, the arguments began. They were small at first, petty disagreements that seemed absurd looking back—so absurd they almost feel comical now. But eventually, things escalated. One day, we reached a breaking point, and just like that, it was over.

When the dust settled, I was left with a bitterness that felt insurmountable—anger toward him, toward myself, even toward God. Why did life have to be so complicated? I had poured so much of myself into that relationship that, in the end, I barely recognized who I was without him. I'd wrapped my entire identity around him, and when it all unraveled, I was left with an emptiness that felt impossible to fill. God was urging me to look forward, to trust that there was something beyond this heartbreak. Yet all I could see was a fog of resentment and regret. It felt as if I'd wasted precious years chasing something that was never meant to last.

I blamed him for it all. I thought he'd taken my youth, my love, my time—leaving me wondering if I could ever love again. In my mind, he was at fault. Every memory seemed to reinforce that narrative: his indifference, his lack of understanding, his inability to meet my needs. I painted him as the villain, blind to my own role in the downward spiral of our love.

It was easier to blame him than to confront the truth. In my desire to hold onto my resentment, I overlooked the fact that relationships are complex, and that our issues weren't his alone. The fights, the frustration—they were as much a reflection of my insecurities and unmet expectations as they were of his. By clinging to the idea that he was the sole cause of our breakup, I could avoid facing my own flaws. If he was the problem, I didn't have to deal with my mistakes. But that mindset, as comforting as it was, only kept me imprisoned in my pain.

And then, in the quiet of my heart, God began to reveal the truth I'd been avoiding love is never one-sided. I had crafted a story where he was the villain, and I was the victim, but that version of events left me powerless, trapped in a cycle of blame. It meant that forgiveness wasn't an option for me because forgiveness would require humility, a willingness to see my own reflection in the brokenness. God was calling me to let go, to surrender the hurt, but I resisted. My bitterness felt like protection, a barrier that kept me from being vulnerable again. Yet that very wall was isolating me, keeping me trapped in my own pain.

The lesson I came to understand through this painful journey was that I was never truly alone. All those years when I was desperately trying to make that relationship work, to fill the emptiness I felt inside, I hadn't realized that God was closer than I ever imagined. I had looked to another person to complete me, to fill the void I carried in my heart. But no human could carry that weight. The peace, the wholeness I sought—those things were only ever going to come from God. He was with me all along, waiting patiently as I searched for love and validation in all the wrong places. I'd sought healing through human hands, but what I needed was a divine embrace, a love that would never let me go.

Forgiveness, I learned, is a difficult and often painful process. It demands that we confront not only the hurts we've endured but also the hurts we've caused. And the closer someone is to our heart, the harder it is to let go of the wounds they leave behind. We expect so much from those we love, believing they should never hurt us because they know us so deeply. And when they fail, it feels like a betrayal. But God was showing me that I needed to see the whole picture—the ways we had both been hurt, both fallen short.

Releasing the bitterness felt impossible, and yet, God continued to invite me into forgiveness, not to dismiss the pain but to free me from it. "Bring him to me," God whispered, His voice steady and gentle, a reminder of all the times I had come before Him with my burdens, seeking healing and peace. I remembered the first time I'd forgiven in His presence, the sense of freedom that came with surrendering my pride and anger. And I realized that this forgiveness wasn't just for him—it was for me. It was a step toward reclaiming my life, toward stepping out of the shadow of bitterness and back into the light of God's grace.

Now, as I reflect on that journey, I am filled with gratitude, knowing that God's strength carried me when I was weakest, that His love filled the emptiness no human could fill. I learned that no matter how deep the pain, God is always there, patient and steady, ready to heal the wounds that others leave behind. Holding onto my hurt only imprisoned me; surrendering it to God set me free. In His hands, the shattered pieces of my heart became whole again, reminding me that with Him, I am never truly alone.

Exodus 20:3-6

You must not have any other god but me. You must not make for yourself an idol of any kind or an image of anything in the heavens or on the earth or in the sea. ⁵ You must not bow down to them or worship them, for I, the Lord your God, am a jealous God who will not tolerate your affection for any other gods. I lay the sins of the parents upon their children; the entire family is affected—even children in the third and fourth generations of those who reject me. ⁶ But I lavish unfailing love for a thousand generations on those who love me and obey my commands.

Here, God commands His people to have no other gods before Him and to refrain from making idols, emphasizing that He is a jealous God. This speaks to God's deep desire for our undivided devotion and love, a devotion that can only be found when we place Him at the center of our hearts. At the time, I didn't realize that I had made an idol out of my relationship. In my desperate search to fill the void of loneliness, I placed all my hope and worth in another person. I thought that if I could just find love from someone else, it would complete me and make me whole, but in doing so, I unknowingly pushed God aside.

I made my relationship the focal point of my life, elevating it above everything—including God. I believed that this person could satisfy the longings in my heart, that their love could heal the emptiness I was feeling. But no matter how hard I tried, I always found myself coming up short, feeling more lost and empty. The truth is, nothing or no one could fill the space that was meant for God alone. As God warns in the passage, placing anything or anyone in His rightful place stirs His righteous jealousy—not because He is insecure, but because He knows that only He can fulfill the deepest desires of our hearts.

When we seek fulfillment outside of Him, we deprive ourselves of the very thing we need most:

His presence. It was only when I stopped relying on someone else to complete me and began to focus my heart back on God that I began to feel whole again. Only He can provide the satisfaction we're all searching for, and when we give Him His rightful place, we experience the fulfillment that nothing else can offer.

Reflection questions:

1. Reflect on a time when you experienced deep hurt from someone. As you revisit that moment, take a step back and ask yourself: what might the Holy Spirit be revealing to you about your own role in that situation and any hurt you may have caused in return?

2. How can you tell when something or someone has become an idol in your life, demanding more of your time, energy, or

affection than it should? How might you redirect your focus back to God and reclaim the devotion and trust that rightly belong to Him?

3. When you reflect on your life, who or what has subtly taken the place of God in your heart? Have you placed someone or something—whether a relationship, career, or material possession—on a pedestal, hoping it would bring you the fulfillment only God can provide?

4. If you were to take an honest look at your life right now, where do you find yourself seeking worth and validation outside of God? How has this affected your relationship with Him, and what steps can you take to realign your heart with His purpose and calling?

ESCAPE

It's astonishing how often we attempt to escape—escape from our past, our pain, and sometimes everything around us, more often than we care to admit. The truth is, we are often trying to escape from ourselves. We harbor a small, persistent wish that we could shed parts of ourselves like snakes shedding their skin. If only we could peel away the aspects we find ugly, the parts that carry the weight of regret and sorrow.

We want to shed our skin, our memories, and our pain. We long for a sense of freedom, to reclaim the innocence we once had, to feel that same excitement for life and thirst for adventure we remember from our youth. We dream of seeing life in vibrant colors once again, not through the murky taints and stains left by our bitter experiences. These experiences have clouded our vision, making it hard to see the beauty and possibilities that once seemed so abundant. We yearn for genuine laughter, the kind that bubbles up from deep within and isn't tinged with bitterness or regret.

But what brings us to this point? What is it that drives us to such lengths to escape? Perhaps it's the accumulation of disappointments, the weight of unfulfilled dreams, or the scars left by past hurts. Life's challenges can be relentless, and over time, they can erode our spirit and dim our outlook. We find ourselves burdened by the residue of these experiences, each one adding a layer of heaviness that makes it harder to see the world with fresh eyes.

We start to question our worth, our decisions, and the path we've taken. The vibrant, hopeful person we once were feels distant, almost like a stranger. We long to reconnect with that part of ourselves, to rediscover the joy and wonder we once felt so naturally. We wish to laugh freely again, without the shadow of past pains lurking in the background.

X.

The night of June 16th, 2019, is a date forever burned into my soul, a night I will never be able to forget. That night, I had a dream so vivid and terrifying that it still lingers in my mind, as clear as if I had just seen it again yesterday. I've often wondered why that dream came to me the way it did, why it unfolded with such intensity. It wasn't just any dream—it was the kind that grips you by the heart and never lets go.

In the dream, I found myself walking down a hallway, a long, dim corridor that felt both familiar and distant. I couldn't shake the feeling that I was searching for something—no, someone. That someone was my father. I pushed open a door, and as soon as I stepped into the room, I saw him. But he wasn't alone.

Standing there was a man I recognized instantly. He wasn't just some random figure from my past—he was one of my father's closest friends, a man who had been like family to us. They were so close that my father had even named one of my siblings after him. They were brothers in everything but blood. I never imagined I would see them like this.

What I saw next sent waves of horror through me. My father's friend had a thick chain wrapped around my father's neck, pulling it tight with all his strength. My father's face was twisted in pain and fear. His friend—this man who had been like a brother—seemed oblivious to my presence, but my father saw me. His eyes locked onto mine, and in that moment, I was paralyzed. I couldn't move. I couldn't speak. The scene before me was so shocking, so unreal, that my body betrayed me. I just stood there, frozen in place, a silent observer.

My father was struggling, his hands desperately trying to keep the chain from choking the life out of him. And yet, even in his agony, he used one hand to gesture to me—telling me without words to stay back, to not come closer. It was as if he was still trying to protect me, even when he was the one in danger.

Tears streamed down my face, but I remained motionless. The words I wanted to say, the plea that rose in my throat—"Stop!" "Leave my dad alone!"—never left my lips. My mind couldn't fully grasp what was happening. It was too much. Then, in the midst of that terrifying scene, my father spoke.

"Promise me," he said, his voice hoarse and strained. "No matter what happens, always keep your faith." His words were filled with urgency, almost as if this promise were more important to him than his own life. "Try God. Try Jesus. I promise you, you will never be disappointed. You need to promise me." He kept repeating it, his words growing more desperate until finally, I whispered my agreement. I promise. And the moment I did, it was as if an invisible force pushed me out of the dream, ejecting me from that horrific scene. Just before I awoke, I saw my father's body relax, as though he had finally let go.

I woke up with a start, gasping for air, my heart racing in my chest. The dream was so real, so visceral, that it took me a moment to realize I was no longer trapped in that room. I sat up, still shaken, and whispered a prayer. I begged God to protect my father, to keep him safe from harm. But even as I prayed, a part of me dismissed the fear. My father was a strong man. He had been through so much in life, and I couldn't imagine that anything, even this, could truly harm him. So, I said a short prayer and tried to shake off the lingering unease.

But that unease clung to me all morning as I went about my day. My father had tried to call me earlier that day, along with some of my siblings, but none of us had picked up—except for one of my brothers, the one born right after me. Something about the missed call gnawed at me, leaving me restless. Eventually, I decided to go home.

As soon as I pulled into the driveway, I saw a friend waiting by the stairs to my apartment. My heart immediately sank. This friend was not the type to just drop by unannounced. Something was wrong. I didn't even ask why he was there—I simply invited him in. His presence was unsettling, and it felt like he was trying to distract me from something. But I didn't want distractions. I wanted answers.

When I went upstairs, I saw my brother pacing in the living room. That sight alone sent alarm bells ringing in my head. This brother, of all my siblings, was the one who never showed fear or anxiety. He had an unwavering faith that I could never understand, a kind of peace that always baffled me. But that day, he looked shaken, and I had never seen him like that.

"What's wrong?" I asked, my voice trembling. He just kept repeating the same words, over and over. "We need to pray for Dad." His tone was so unfamiliar, so strained, that I couldn't make sense of it. I went into my room to pray, I sat near the window facing outside, As soon as I sat, the truth hit me like a freight train. I knew, deep inside, that my father was not okay. Something had happened.

Then it felt like a covering was lifted from me and I was suddenly exposed; A strange thing that felt so spiritual I don't know how to put it into words. I prayed harder, more desperately than I ever had before. "God, I know I haven't been the best Christian, but please, if you save my dad, I'll change. I'll get my life together." But even as I prayed, I felt something leave me—like a piece of my soul was being torn away. It was as if I already knew the answer before I even asked.

My father was gone.

A deep sadness enveloped me, so overwhelming that I could hardly breathe. But I didn't want to believe it. I pushed the feeling down, refusing to acknowledge it. I needed to get out of the house. I needed air. So, I left my room and went downstairs, passing my friend without a word.

When I stepped outside, I was met with the sight of more friends arriving, gathering outside my apartment. Most of them I hadn't seen in ages, and they all had that same look in their eyes. They kept saying the same thing: "Be strong." Every time I heard those words, I felt my anger rise. Why were they telling me that? What did they know that I didn't?

Their words, their pity, their looks—all of it made me furious. It was as if their concern was making my worst fears real. I wanted to scream at them to stop, to leave me alone. I couldn't bear the thought of what they were implying. If they kept talking, if they kept looking at me like that, it would mean that everything I was feeling—everything I was afraid of—was true.

I couldn't accept it. I wouldn't. My father couldn't die. Not him. Not now. Not like this.

I wanted to run. I wanted to escape. But there was nowhere to go. The feelings inside me were too powerful, too raw to outrun. I felt trapped inside my own skin, suffocated by the weight of it all. I wanted to peel it all away, to tear myself apart, to release the agony that was building up inside me. I wanted to scream. I wanted to punch something, to break something, to make the pain stop. But more than anything, I wanted to wake up. This had to be another dream. It couldn't be real. Not this. Not me.

"God, where are you?" I cried out silently, desperately searching for some sense of peace, some escape from the crushing reality that was closing in on me. But there was none. There was only emptiness. And in that emptiness, I realized I couldn't disappear, no matter how much I wanted to.

I couldn't stop thinking, "I should have prayed more. I should have picked up the call. I should have tried to protect him, or at least done something—anything. Why did I underestimate death? Why did I overestimate my dad? Why did I believe he was stronger than death itself?"

These thoughts haunted me. "I didn't even get to say goodbye. "The crushing sadness of knowing my dad died alone, with no one by his side, consumed me. He breathed his last breath alone, and that thought paralyzed me. At some point, I even found myself angry at him. I couldn't help but feel that if only I had known things were bad, I could have done something. I was angry because, when things got hard, he didn't let me, or the rest of our family love him. He didn't give us the chance to stand by him and support him in his final moments.

No matter what I did, I couldn't shake these feelings. I kept thinking about the memories we'd never create the pictures we never took, the questions I never asked. All the things he was going to miss. I hadn't seen him in four years, "why didn't I go back just once, to be with him, to spend time with him? "I felt lost, sad, confused. It seemed like there was no way out of grief.

But I had to stay strong. I had younger siblings to think about, and my mom—oh, my mom, I had to be strong for her. I didn't want her to worry about me.

Job 1:21

When Job heard this, he tore his clothes and shaved his head because of his great sorrow. He knelt on the ground, then worshiped God and said: "We bring nothing at birth; we take nothing with us at death. The LORD alone gives and takes. Praise the name of the LORD!

Have you experienced a loss that left a lasting mark on your soul? Loss comes in many forms — the passing of a loved one, the end of a relationship, the unraveling of a dream, or even the loss of who you once were. These moments can leave us shaken to our core, raw and exposed, with questions that often feel too big to answer. Grief has a way of stripping us down to the most vulnerable parts of ourselves, forcing us to confront the fragility of the things we hold dear.

Job utters words of profound surrender. His response challenges us to consider the nature of everything we have — our loved ones, our achievements, and even our very lives. All are entrusted to us by God, not as possessions to cling to, but as gifts to steward. When loss strikes, it's easy to feel as though our world is unraveling. Yet, Job's words remind us that even in the face of devastation, there is space to honor God, acknowledging His sovereignty over both the giving and the taking.

This doesn't mean the pain of loss is any less real or that grief becomes easier to bear. Instead, Job's response invites us into a posture of faith — a faith that doesn't deny the anguish but trusts in God's ultimate goodness, even when life feels anything but good. It's a faith that whispers, *"I don't understand, but I trust You."* It's in these moments of surrender, when we release the clenched fists of control and offer our pain to God, that we begin to find a strange and sacred kind of peace.

Loss changes us, but it doesn't have to destroy us. It has the power to deepen our trust in God, to remind us that our hope isn't rooted in the temporary but in the eternal. Job's story shows us that faith is not the absence of pain but the willingness to hold onto God in the midst of it, trusting that He is with us and for us, even in our darkest hours.

Reflection questions:

1. Are there areas of your life where you've struggled to see loss as a part of God's greater purpose? How might trusting in His ultimate goodness help you find peace in circumstances that feel chaotic or senseless?

2. Loss often leaves us asking, "Why?" but Job chose to trust God without fully understanding. How do you respond when God's plan doesn't align with your expectations? Are you willing to trade your need for answers for a deeper faith in His goodness?

3. Loss has a way of revealing where we place our ultimate hope. As you reflect on Job's story, where do you see God inviting you to trust Him more deeply, even if it means letting go of something you once thought you couldn't live without?

4. How might recognizing God as both the giver and sustainer of life reshape the way you hold onto the things and people you cherish? What would it mean for you to entrust everything to Him, even in the face of uncertainty?

Dear God,

I've been thinking about my dad all day. Some days are harder than others, but today feels especially heavy. I'd give anything to sit with him again, just to hear him laugh or watch the way he looked at life. He had this quiet wisdom; he never told me how to live, he just showed me through every choice he made. I wonder if he ever realized how much I was watching, how much I was learning, even in the simplest moments.

Everywhere I go, there are pieces of him. I hear his voice in the back of my mind when I'm faced with a choice or when things get tough. And it's strange – how can someone who's gone feel so close, yet so far? I can still feel the strength of his love, like an anchor holding me steady, even when it hurts to think he is no longer here.

But I know this: love doesn't fade. The ache is real, but so is the love, and somehow, even in the silence, it's like he is still beside me. I don't have the words to explain it, but I feel it. Every tear, every memory, it's a reminder of the price of loving him so deeply. And maybe that's why it hurts so much – because he meant that much.

I miss you, Daddy.

More than words can say.

XI.

You might ask me, what caused my father's death? Well, the truth is, he was killed. Found dead in his hotel room. Just like that. One moment he was alive, the next, I was receiving the news that shattered my world. The call came out of nowhere, and the words that followed felt like a blur, as if the whole world slowed down. I couldn't comprehend what I was hearing. My father—this strong, reliable, loving figure who had always been there—was gone. It didn't make sense. I had so many questions, but no answers. How could something like this happen to someone like him? How could it be so sudden, so final?

Before I could even process the grief, the ground beneath me gave way again. My mother, in the midst of all this chaos, was poisoned. The shock of losing my father hadn't even settled, and now, my mother was unconscious, her life hanging by a thread. She remained in a coma for two long weeks, and during that time, I could feel myself drowning. Everything was happening so fast, too fast for my mind to keep up. My family, my world, was crumbling, and all I could do was watch, helpless and alone.

When my mother finally woke, we hoped, we prayed, that things would start to calm down. But peace was nowhere to be found. In fact, it was as if a storm was just beginning. The legal battles over my father's body were the next crushing blow. As if the loss of a loved one wasn't enough, now there were people fighting over him, disputing his right to be claimed. They refused to release his body to my mother. She had already lost her husband; now she had to fight just to give him a proper burial. It was as though his death wasn't the end of the trauma, but the beginning of another war. Bureaucracy became a tool for further devastation, and it felt like the injustice of it all was just piling on.

Eventually, my mother won that battle. But it didn't end there. The threats, the intimidation, started coming—dark, anonymous letters that smelled of danger. The kind of forces we couldn't see but could feel creeping into every part of our lives. Fear became our constant companion. We no longer felt safe in our own home. My mother, devastated and now in constant danger, made the painful decision to leave our country with my younger siblings. The place we once called home had become a prison. My mother's fight for survival had turned into a daily battle. The country, where women's rights were often ignored, was no longer a place of refuge for her, for us.

At that time, I was far away in Philadelphia, thousands of miles apart, but the pain of helplessness and guilt consumed me. I felt like an outsider in my own life, watching everything fall apart from a distance. The guilt weighed on me like a thousand pounds. If only I had prayed more, if only I had done something differently, maybe my father would still be here. If I had been there for my mother, for my younger siblings, maybe things would have turned out differently. But all I could do was stand by, feeling powerless. I couldn't save him. I couldn't save my family. I couldn't fix anything.

And then, to add to the chaos, my long-term relationship—something I had always thought was stable—shattered. It was like God had turned on me, throwing every possible weight onto my shoulders. Sometimes I wonder if I should have seen it coming. But I was a girl in love, lost in a fairy tale. When it ended, it felt like I was falling through an endless void. There was no way out, no escape from the hurt, no one to catch me. The world seemed to collapse around me. Broken, desperate, I just wanted to run. Run from everything. Run from the pain.

Then, just as my personal life was crumbling, the world shut down. COVID-19 hit, and we were all forced into isolation. As an introvert, I initially welcomed the quiet. It felt like a reprieve from the chaos. But the silence soon became suffocating. My thoughts grew darker and darker, haunting me in those lonely hours. I couldn't escape them. All I could think about was my family—my father's death, my mother's condition, the chaos I couldn't control. The quiet wasn't peaceful; it was a reminder of everything I couldn't fix, everything I couldn't change.

One memory from that time stands out so vividly that I'll never forget it. I was completely alone in my apartment. The weight of everything was suffocating me, and that day had been especially hard. It was as though the reality of my father's death hit me all over again, but this time with an intensity that left me gasping for breath. I truly thought that night might be the end for me. In that moment, I felt so far removed from everything, so distant from the world, that I believed my only way out was to end it all. I even wrote a note to my mom, thinking it would give her peace if I didn't make it through the night. I remember how delusional that felt now—how selfish I was, only thinking of myself when she had just lost her husband. She couldn't bear the loss of a daughter, too.

I unlocked every door in my apartment—every single one, even the front door. I thought that if I died, someone would find me. And then, almost as if God had heard my silent cry, I got a text from one of my dearest friends. At the time, She was just someone I had known from church, a girl I'd connected with, but in that moment, she was a lifeline. She said she was coming over to see me. I didn't even remember replying. I was so numb. But moments later, I heard the door open and footsteps approaching my bedroom. She didn't say a word. I don't even think I looked up at her. She just sat beside me, close enough to feel her presence, her warmth. And in that silence, I began to cry uncontrollably.

"He's not coming back, is he? He's never coming back," I sobbed, my tears pouring down without stopping. She didn't try to comfort me with words, didn't tell me it would be okay. She just stayed there with me, crying with me. For the first time in a long time, I felt like I wasn't alone. She held me, and for some reason, that act of simply being there—being present—was a balm to my aching soul. The sense of death that had been looming over me began to fade, and in its place was a tiny flicker of hope.

After a long while, she stood up and gently said, "You're coming with me." I didn't argue. I just got up, and we went to her place. She gave me her bed to sleep in, and I slept so soundly that night, as if the weight of the world had been lifted, if only for a few hours. The next morning, she made me a meal—a simple dish of rice—but it's one I'll never forget. It was the taste of comfort, of care, of a love that went beyond words

That's how I escaped death that night. I don't know if I would have made it through without her. Later, when I asked her what had made her come over that day, she said she had a feeling in her heart that she should stop by, even if only for a little while. And when she said that it hit me: God had been watching over me.

In that moment, I realized that my time hadn't come yet. I wasn't alone, even when I thought I was. I was so grateful for that gift of life, even as I struggled with the anger and confusion still lingering in my heart. The tension between gratitude and anger was palpable, but in the quiet aftermath of that night, I understood that God was still with me, still protecting me, still holding me together when I thought I was falling apart.

Isaiah 41:10

Don't you be afraid, for I am with you. Don't be dismayed, for I am your God. I will strengthen you. Yes, I will help you. Yes, I will uphold you with the right hand of my righteousness

In moments of deep grief and despair, it's easy to feel utterly abandoned, as if the weight of the world has crushed us beyond repair. Yet, Isaiah 41:10 reminds us that we are never truly alone, even when the darkness feels unbearable. God's invitation to "not fear" is not a dismissal of our pain but a compassionate promise to meet us in it. His presence is not distant or passive—it is active and unrelenting, a source of strength when we feel weakest and a foundation when everything around us seems to crumble.

There are times when life feels unbearable, like when you sit alone in the quiet of your room, surrounded by the ache of loss or fear. But even in those moments, God is there. His righteous right hand upholds you, even when you feel like you're falling. He sends lifelines in ways we don't always recognize at first—a call from a friend, a word of encouragement, or a sense of peace that surpasses understanding.

This promise is not dependent on your strength, but on His. You don't have to hold yourself together, because He is the one holding you. When fear threatens to paralyze you and despair whispers that you are alone, remember that God is already at work, strengthening you and guiding you forward. His love is the safety net that catches you when you fall and the firm ground that steadies you when you rise. Trust in His promise—He is with you always, offering His unwavering support and strength to help you carry on.

Reflection Questions:

1. Reflect on a time when someone showed up for you in your darkest moment. How might this have been God's way of reminding you of His presence and care? How can you stay open to recognizing His interventions, even when they come in unexpected forms?

2. Think about the people God has placed in your life who have been His hands and feet during your times of struggle. How can you follow their example and be a source of comfort and support to others in their moments of need?

3. What does it mean to you personally that God's "righteous right hand" is upholding

you? Take a moment to reflect on the imagery of God's hand — strong, steady, and unwavering — holding you up when you feel like you're falling. How does this truth reshape the way you view your struggles, knowing that you are not relying on your own strength but on His limitless power?

4. In what ways can this promise bring you peace and assurance, especially in times of uncertainty or Grief, etc. ? How might fully embracing this truth help you face life's challenges with greater confidence, trusting that God is not only with you but actively sustaining you through it all?

Father

It's hard to even write to You right now. There was a time when I could talk to You about everything. But when You took my daddy away, You broke something in me. I did not just lose him—I lost You, too. I am so angry. I don't know how to be close to You anymore, and honestly, I'm not sure I want to.

I looked to him as the one steady, unshakable part of my life. He was my rock, and You took him. Why? Did You think I don't need him anymore? Because I still do; I need him so much I feel the ache, God, every day; the emptiness left behind where his presence used to fill my heart.

Sometimes it feels like there's a wall between you and me now—one that I don't know how to climb.

I miss those quiet moments when I could just sit with You, when I did not question if You cared or if You were even listening. Now, even finding the words feels like a battle. But I guess this is a start, me sitting here, writing out these things I've held back. I'm not even sure if I want an answer; I just want You to know that it hurts. It still hurts, and I don't know what to do with that pain.

God, I don't know if I'm ready for peace or healing. Maybe I'm just here because, deep down, some part of me misses You, even though I'm so mad at You. Maybe I'm hoping You'll understand my silence, my distance.

That You'll find a way to be with me, even when I can't find a way to talk to You.

XII.

God was never a stranger to me—He was constant, present in every corner of our home. He was the melody in the song my father sang at 4 a.m. every day, filling the silence with devotion. God was life itself. My father always directed my siblings and me toward Him. He radiated Christ in such a way that when my mother told me he hadn't always believed, I struggled to accept it. How could that be? It seemed impossible to me. Everyone knew how much he loved God.

In our home, attending every church service wasn't just encouraged, it was a strict rule I once resented. Missing a service was unacceptable, and we would face consequences if we did. There was no room for negotiation, no excuse for absence. Faith was the foundation of our lives—it held our home together, and we were taught to honor it above all else. At the time, I resented it, feeling suffocated by the constant need to show devotion, to be perfect in our obedience.

Faith surrounded me. The reality of God was undeniable; I saw it everywhere. I knew of God before I truly knew Him. He was always there, making His presence known through miracles. I witnessed people being healed, lives transformed, and testimonies of His power. My curiosity grew. Eventually, I started going to church of my own accord, eager to learn more about Him. The more I learned, the more I began to love Him. But my love was imperfect—rooted in what He could do for me rather than who He truly is.

I knew God as a healer, a miracle worker, a provider—the one who blesses and gives. Yet, I had not experienced Him beyond these roles. He was the one who answered prayers, who made everything right when things went wrong, but I had not yet encountered Him in His fullness—His mysterious, unsearchable nature, or His willingness to allow suffering for reasons I couldn't yet understand.

During this time, when all these events were unfolding, I began to wonder about God. I questioned His intentions and actions toward me. Was He trying to deepen my understanding of Him? To stretch my faith in ways I wasn't prepared for. Why was His hand so heavy upon me, pressing me in ways that felt unbearable?

I wrestled with my thoughts, trying to reconcile the God I'd been taught to love with the God I was encountering in my own life. His silence left me hollow, and I found myself questioning everything. Was it a test of faith? Was I being punished for some hidden wrongdoing? Could I have done something to cause this pain? The questions gnawed at me. But then, I started to wonder: could there really be a sin so great that He couldn't forgive it? Could my failures, my shortcomings, really make me so undeserving of His grace? Was it that I didn't pray enough, or pray the right way?

I remember how my older siblings used to challenge me when we were younger, telling me I should be able to pray for at least two hours straight—a feat I had never managed. They could, but I couldn't. Was this what God expected of me as a Christian? To meet a standard that felt so far beyond my reach. I had always been the one who struggled to focus, to stay engaged in the rituals of faith, and now it felt like my very soul was failing the test.

I resented Him. Deep down, I harbored this anger, feeling as though God was some kind of tyrant—unmovable, uncaring, a force that did whatever He wanted, regardless of how it affected fragile beings like me. He knew how weak I was. Why, then, would He take advantage of my frailty? Why would He burden me with more than I could bear? I began to see Him not as a loving Father, but as an all-powerful judge who held lives in His hands and decided, at His whim, who would suffer and who would be spared. I hated that feeling. It wasn't just confusion; it was a deep, gnawing resentment that took root in my heart.

I tried going to church, but only because of the promise I had made to my father that night in the dream. I was going through the motions, my heart not in it. Yet every time I stepped through those doors, a wave of anger washed over me—a level of rage I had never experienced before. I hated Him. I didn't want anything to do with God anymore. To me, He was mean, selfish. Did He even answer prayers the way people claimed He did? Or was it all just a cruel game? Why did He toy with my heart like that? Why would He allow something to happen that shook the very ground beneath me? My heart was a battlefield, and I was losing the war.

When my father passed, everything changed. My father was my rock. My strength. He was the anchor in the storm, the one who could always bring peace with a word, who could calm the chaos of my thoughts with just his presence. And then, God took him from me. I couldn't understand it. I still can't. For God to take him from me the way He did—so suddenly, so painfully—felt like the ultimate betrayal. How was I supposed to move forward after that?

I was left adrift, grasping at the pieces of my shattered faith, but they wouldn't fit together anymore. Every prayer felt like a lie, every word hollow.

In my anger, I started to fear God as well. He was this powerful being who held life itself in His hands, capable of ending my existence with just a breath. I became hyper-aware of His greatness, His might, and it terrified me. He was beyond understanding, capable of doing anything—and that realization only deepened my fear.

I couldn't even comprehend how, in the midst of my anger and resentment, I could still see Him for the powerful being He was. I feared what He could do to me, even as I resented the fact that He could do anything at all. What was the point of praying anymore? Did my faith even matter?

Was there any reason to keep pretending to be this "good Christian," obeying the laws of the Bible, when God was just going to do whatever He wanted anyway? I was convinced there was no point in trying anymore. My prayers felt hollow, my faith meaningless. I didn't believe He was listening. I didn't believe He cared.

I cried out to Him, "If You're planning to do something else as tragic, as devastating as this, then please take me too. Don't leave me here in this pain." I even considered ending it all myself, though the only thing stopping me was the knowledge that it would be a sin.

Still, I begged Him—since He was God, couldn't He just let me go? Couldn't He let me fall asleep and never wake again? Death started to seem like the only escape. I believed it could free me from this world, from the unbearable weight of grief and the torment of living in a world where God, the devil, pain, and responsibilities all felt like chains around my soul.

In death, I thought, I could finally be free.

Mathew 11:28-30

Then Jesus said, "Come to me, all of you who are weary and carry heavy burdens, and I will give you rest. Take my yoke upon you. Let me teach you, because I am humble and gentle at heart, and you will find rest for your souls. For my yoke is easy to bear, and the burden I give you is light."

In the midst of pain, anger, and grief, it can be easy to feel like we're carrying a weight too heavy to bear. Life often leaves us feeling like we're walking through a storm without an anchor, and in those moments, God may seem distant or unmovable, just as you may have felt in the hardest chapters of your journey. The questions swirl—why is this happening, and where is God in the midst of it? Yet, in Matthew 11:28-30, Jesus extends an invitation that cuts through the noise of our suffering: "Come to me, all you who are weary and burdened, and I will give you rest."

This rest goes deeper than physical relief or a temporary reprieve from struggle. It's a rest rooted in His gentle and compassionate nature, a rest that meets us in the depths of our weariness and reminds us that we don't have to carry our burdens alone. Jesus doesn't promise to take away every challenge, but He offers us something infinitely more profound—a yoke that is easy, a burden that is light, and the assurance that He walks with us every step of the way.

Even when we feel distant from God, overwhelmed by the weight of our pain, this verse reminds us that He is closer than we realize. He doesn't demand perfection, polished prayers, or an understanding of why we are suffering. Instead, He calls us to come to Him exactly as we are, brokenness and all. His promise is not to shame us for our struggles but to gently guide us toward healing and wholeness, offering the kind of rest that quiets our souls and renews our hope.

God's rest is an invitation to release the burden of trying to figure everything out or hold ourselves together. It's an invitation to lean into His unchanging love, trusting that He will carry us in ways we could never carry ourselves. In Him, we find not only rest but also the reassurance that even in our confusion, pain, and weakness, we are held, seen, and deeply loved.

Reflection Questions:

1. Reflect on the burdens you've been carrying—whether emotional, mental, or spiritual. How has trying to carry these burdens alone affected your peace or sense of well-being? How does Jesus' invitation to rest offer a new perspective on dealing with these struggles?

2. Think about the areas of your life where you've felt overwhelmed or exhausted. How does the promise of Jesus offering "rest for your souls" speak to the deep weariness that may come from trying to manage everything by your own strength?

3. Consider the idea of taking Jesus' yoke upon you—allowing His gentleness and humility to guide your life. What might it

look like for you to lean into His leadership, trusting that His way will bring you peace rather than burdening you further?

4. Think about the things you've been seeking to fill the emptiness or exhaustion in your soul. How might inviting Jesus into those places of weariness change how you experience rest and peace? What practical steps can you take to surrender those burdens to Him and find true rest in His presence?

Ungrounded

A strange feeling of being here but not here at the same time. As if I live in some sort of paradox where everything moves both swiftly and sluggishly, blurring the edges of reality. What's happening? I feel like a feather caught in the capricious wind, drifting aimlessly with no direction or purpose.

Ungrounded

How did I get here? Where was I going with that train of thought? Who was I talking to? Are they telling me the truth? My mind is a maze of fragmented thoughts and unanswered questions. Who am I again?

Scattered

I don't know what's happening to me. Every joy and every passion is fleeting. I can feel them slip through my fingers, one by one, until they completely disappear, leaving me here once more, searching for something—

anything—that feels real and substantial. Something I can't quite grasp.

Unbalanced, disoriented

Where is my anchor? I need to be anchored, to find some solid ground in this whirlwind of uncertainty. I long for stability, for something to hold onto that will keep me from being swept away.

God where are you?

XIII.

In my desperation to escape the suffocating weight of my life, I packed my bags one day and left Philadelphia. I ran—fast and far—all the way to Kansas, believing that the quiet and emptiness I hoped to find would drown out the relentless noise in my mind. It was an attempt to outrun my pain, a search for peace in a place I thought would offer a fresh start.

I threw myself into work and school, juggling multiple jobs while studying full-time, keeping myself so busy that I barely had a moment to think about the grief I carried. But no matter how hard I tried to fill the silence with distractions, the nightmares followed. Every night, I was haunted by visions of my father's death—cold, alone, abandoned.

His final moments replayed in vivid detail, breaking my heart over and over again. And when I awoke, it was to an all-consuming emptiness, as though the world around me had gone silent, leaving me to drown in my own sorrow.

The weight of grief began to take a toll on my body. Stomach ulcers flared, heartburn gnawed at me, and anxiety attacks became an almost constant companion. I would tremble uncontrollably, overwhelmed by the terror that I was losing my mind. But it wasn't just my body that was failing me. It was my spirit, too. The grief, the isolation, the crushing loneliness—all of it had made me question if I would ever find peace again.

In the quiet moments, when everything else was still, a familiar voice crept in again. That same dark whisper that had plagued me before, the one that urged me to give up: "Kill yourself." The thought seemed to promise an escape, a release from the unbearable weight of everything I couldn't change. The idea lingered, relentless, pulling at me like an undertow I couldn't escape.

My family's situation remained unchanged, the grief was unrelenting, and every night I struggled to find rest. As a foreigner in the U.S., the stress of living in a country that often felt alien made everything harder to bear. Some days, the thought of death seemed like the only option to find peace.

Then, one day, during a particularly overwhelming class, I broke down. My professor noticed and approached me after the class ended. For the first time in a long time, I allowed myself to speak the truth about what I was going through, sharing only pieces of the overwhelming weight I carried. She listened. She didn't try to fix it or tell me everything would be fine, but she urged me to seek help. It was a lifeline, one I hadn't realized I needed. Hesitant, but desperate, I began therapy at my college.

The counselor I saw didn't rush to offer solutions, but she created a safe space where I could begin to confront the depth of my pain. She helped me understand that healing isn't instantaneous. After a few sessions, she then referred me to a specialist, and it wasn't long before I received a diagnosis that left me reeling—chronic anxiety, severe depression, and PTSD. The words felt like chains, like labels that defined me, deepening my confusion and despair. How had I ended up here?

They felt like chains—chains that tightened around me with every syllable, constricting my ability to breathe or think clearly. It was as though these labels were being handed to me, but they didn't quite fit. They seemed foreign, as if I were hearing a language I didn't understand. PTSD? How could that be? I hadn't witnessed the traumatic events firsthand. I hadn't been in the room when my father died. I hadn't physically seen my mother fight for her life. So how could I have PTSD? It didn't make sense. I thought trauma was only for those who had directly experienced something violent or horrifying. But here they were—words I didn't fully understand, dropped into my lap, and it was up to me to figure out how they applied to me, how they could possibly be a part of my story.

I couldn't help but wonder if I had missed something, if there were pieces of the puzzle I hadn't seen or understood. It felt like being handed a book written in a language I didn't speak, and I was left trying to decode it on my own. These terms—these diagnoses—seemed to point to something I didn't know how to confront. They were not just words on paper. They were the definition of my reality, but I couldn't figure out how they connected to the life I had lived. How had I ended up here, in this place of profound suffering, when it seemed like I hadn't experienced what others would call trauma in the usual sense?

As much as I resisted the labels, they lingered. They haunted me, becoming part of how I viewed myself, even though I couldn't fully grasp what they meant. But now, it felt like these words were wrapping themselves around me, forcing me to confront parts of myself I wasn't ready to face. How could I make sense of something that didn't seem to make sense at all?

The thought of taking medication terrified me. If I took the pills, it would mean that everything I had been feeling was real. It felt like giving up, like surrendering to the mess that had overtaken my life.

I had always hoped for a miracle, something that would change my circumstances without having to face the depth of my pain. But deep down, I knew I couldn't keep pretending that I was fine. The weight of my grief, my anxiety, and my fear of facing my brokenness had become too much to bear alone. So, reluctantly, I took the first step toward healing, opening myself up to the possibility that God might be able to help me in ways I hadn't imagined.

I was exhausted—physically, mentally, and spiritually. Every day felt like I was running on empty, holding on just long enough to survive. But the situation felt increasingly out of my control. My father was gone, my family scattered, and the pandemic had isolated me further. I had no home to return to, no clear path forward, and the pressure of maintaining my student visa weighed heavily on me. The world around me felt hostile and cold. I was living in a constant state of survival, not just distraction.

Then, one night, everything came to a head. I collapsed in prayer, alone in my room, feeling utterly empty and lost. "God, this is it," I whispered through tears. "I can't do this anymore. I'm at the end of myself. I can't do this alone." In that moment of raw vulnerability, I felt as if I had been stripped of every facade, every attempt at self-reliance.

There were no excuses left, no pretenses. I was just a broken soul, standing before God, with nothing left but my heart. And as I surrendered in that moment, I sensed His presence in a way I hadn't before. It was as though the weight of the world had been momentarily lifted, and for the first time in a long time, I felt that I was exactly where I needed to be—right in His hands.

The words my brother had spoken to me during a particularly dark time came to mind: **"We don't belong to ourselves. We belong to God."** At the time, I had dismissed his words as a simple Christian platitude, but now, in my brokenness, those words settled deeply in my heart. **We belong to God**. And somehow, that truth brought a peace I couldn't explain. It was like a flicker of light in the darkness. My pain didn't disappear, but in that moment, I knew that I didn't have to carry it alone. God had been with me all along, even when I had doubted His presence.

Psalm 62:5-6

Wait calmly for God alone, my soul, because my hope comes from him. He alone is my rock and my savior-my stronghold. I cannot be shaken

Sometimes, life's burdens can feel like they are slowly breaking us down—physically, emotionally, and spiritually. The weight of stress, anxiety, or loss can manifest in ways we can't ignore: the tightness in our chest, the constant headaches, or the sleepless nights that seem to stretch on forever. We might even feel as though the ground beneath us is shaking, and our grip on control is slipping away.

It's not just our bodies that suffer—the heaviness of our spirits can leave us questioning if peace will ever return. The isolation, the worry, and the relentless pressure can make it feel like we are carrying more than we can bear.

In these moments of exhaustion and uncertainty, Psalm 62:5-6 offers a life-changing reminder: God is our unmovable foundation. His strength, His love, and His promises remain steady even when everything around us feels unstable. When the world is a whirlwind of fear and doubt, God stands as our rock—unchanging, firm, and secure. His presence is a fortress that provides safety in the storm. He invites us to lean into Him, to release our worries, and to rest in the peace that comes from knowing He is our constant source of stability.

When everything else seems to shift or crumble, God's promises are the anchor that keeps us grounded. You are not alone in your struggles; you are anchored in His love and His strength. In the moments when you feel overwhelmed or uncertain, trust that God is with you, holding you steady. Lean into Him, and find the peace that comes from knowing that no matter how fierce the storm, with God as your foundation, you will stand firm through every challenge.

Reflection questions:

1. In what areas of your life do you feel unsettled, vulnerable, or overwhelmed right now? How can you intentionally bring these concerns before God, asking Him to help you find peace and comfort in His presence, trusting that He will guide you through these moments?

2. When you're facing challenges, what does it practically look like for you to "rest in God"? How can you create intentional space for this rest, whether through prayer, reflection, or stillness, and make it a regular part of your daily routine, even amid the demands of life?

3. How can you remind yourself daily that God is your rock and fortress, especially

when life feels uncertain, chaotic, or out of control? What are some specific actions or reminders that can help you focus on His steady, unchanging nature in those moments?

4. Reflecting on a time when you experienced God's steady presence during a difficult moment, what did you learn from that experience? How can that lesson encourage and strengthen you as you face current challenges, helping you to trust in His faithfulness even when things seem tough? How can you shift your focus from your circumstances to the unshakable nature of God's love and faithfulness when life feels overwhelming?

Father,

Reveal Your character to me.

I find myself wandering, trying to control everything, gripped by fear that You won't come through for me. I know in my mind that You are good—I've seen You do amazing things. Yet, I've also witnessed pain and sorrow, and still, You called it good.

And so,

I am afraid.

Afraid because I don't understand what You call good, and I struggle to grasp how something that doesn't feel good can still be within Your plan. Teach me, Lord, to redefine good by Your standards.

Help me believe when You say that the plans You have for me are to prosper me, even when I can't see the path ahead. I long to trust in Your character, even when the outcome is unknown. Come, Lord, reveal Yourself to me and help me trust You more with each passing day.

May my faith, though small as a mustard seed, grow steadily as You show me glimpses of Your face and remind me of Your goodness.

In Jesus' name, I pray.

Amen.

XIV.

I remember one Sunday at church, the sermon focused on the goodness of God. The familiar words of the song "All my life you have been faithful" filled the air as the congregation sang, "I will sing of the goodness of God." But as I stood there, listening, the question nagged at me:

'What goodness?'

How could I believe in the goodness of God when everything in my life felt so wrong? How could I sing about His faithfulness when my heart was heavy with grief and confusion? My mind was flooded with so many questions—'Was life supposed to be this way?' Was I expected to still believe that God was good, even when nothing around me seemed to reflect that?

It felt like a cruel irony, especially as I considered the world beyond me—people who didn't even believe in God- seemingly happy, enjoying life without the constant weight of suffering I carried.

Was this my reward for faith? A life filled with pain. I didn't sign up for this. Why did it seem like my life was a never-ending cycle of heartache, from depression to grief, breakups, and my family being scattered and my own financial struggles? When would it end? Even if God saw me as strong, was I supposed to be this strong? No, I couldn't believe it.

There were days when I felt anything but strong. One day, I scrolled through my WhatsApp profile, and my status boldly read, "I am a strong woman of God, I can handle it." But as I stared at those words, I thought, This is probably what is giving God ideas about me. I wasn't strong. My world was falling apart, and I was losing myself. I felt exhausted, confused, unsure of what would become of me or my family. No one in my family would share the details of what was really happening, telling me they wanted to protect me. But I was drowning in uncertainty. Life felt like a bad nightmare, and I kept waiting to wake up. Nothing made sense. In that place of despair, it was impossible to believe that God was good.

I told myself, Sure, God is good—but not to me. Not to my family. I wrestled with two conflicting questions: Was God not good at all? or had my family committed some hidden sin, and this was His punishment?

I had no answers, only more questions. That day at church, after the worship ended, a man went up to the podium and gave his testimony. I don't remember all the details, but I remember him sharing his story—how he had lost several members of his family within a year or two, a series of tragedies that would break most people. He spoke about a time when he, his wife, and their child had no home, how they had lived in the street struggling just to get by. And yet, as he told it, there was a joy on his face that I couldn't understand, a kind of peace that seemed almost impossible given everything he had endured.

His life was filled with unimaginable hardship, but his joy radiated in a way that shook me. How could someone who had lost so much have that kind of joy? I couldn't keep listening to the rest of his story. I was too overwhelmed by the joy he had in the midst of such chaos. I cried as I sat there, wondering how he could not be mad at God. Why wasn't he angry? How did he not feel cheated? It wasn't just confusion; it was a sense of betrayal.

Here I was, doing my best to remain faithful, and yet I couldn't understand why this man, who had lost more than I could imagine, radiated a peace that seemed out of reach for me. It seemed almost unfair that someone could experience tragedy, and still find joy in God. Was that the kind of faith God expected from me? Was He waiting for me to respond with worship while I was still reeling from everything that had happened?

As much as I wanted answers, I couldn't escape the nagging thought that maybe my struggle was more about my expectations of God rather than His actual nature. Had I built my faith on the idea that God existed to make my life easy, And when that didn't happen, was I quick to assume He wasn't good? I felt torn between wanting to trust

Him and the harsh reality of my circumstances that said otherwise.

Then, my mind wandered back to the story of Job, a man who endured unimaginable suffering yet refused to abandon his faith. I remembered how, as a child, I had fixated on his wife's response to their pain. I couldn't stand her. How could she tell him to curse God and die? Didn't she care about him at all? But now, as I stood in the midst of my own pain, I began to see her differently. I wouldn't say I agreed with her, but I could finally understand where she was coming from, the weight of grief, the frustration, the sense of hopelessness. And yet, something held me back. What stopped me from doing what Job's wife suggested? Why didn't I turn my back on God? Why was I still here, clinging to hope, searching for answers?

I remembered reading in Job that when Job was stripped of everything, his first response was to fall to his knees and worship.

WORSHIP.

How?

His life had just fallen apart. Didn't he feel what I was feeling? What did Job know that I didn't? David's story was the same—amidst his turmoil, he kept worshiping. How could they respond to suffering with such unwavering faith?

In that moment, I realized something shocking: I'd been a Christian all my life, yet it seemed like I didn't really know God at all. Not the way Job and David did, not the way that man at church did.

So many more questions rushed through my mind. Who was God to me? What was I expecting from Him? How was I supposed to relate to a God who allowed so much pain and suffering in my life? And how was it that people like Job, David, and the man at church could go through unimaginable trials and still worship, still believe, still remain faithful? What did they know?

I needed to know what they knew. I needed to make sense of God and my faith. Because right at that moment, I was lost, and the only thing that seemed to hold me was the hope that maybe, just maybe, there were answers beyond my pain.

It all felt stifling, so I stepped outside of the church. I needed space, a moment to breathe. As I stood there, the memory of that dream about my dad flooded my mind-- how he urged me to keep my faith. Of all the things he could have said, he chose those words, as if he knew something I hadn't yet realized.

I started to wonder if he understood just how much his death would impact me, how deeply it would shake my relationship with God, to the point where I wasn't even sure I wanted to continue as a Christian. "Keep your faith," I heard him say again in my mind. Taking a deep breath, I decided to return inside and stay, at least until the service ended.

Daniel 3:17-18

If we are thrown into the blazing furnace, the God we serve is able to deliver us from it, and he will deliver us from Your Majesty's hand. But even if he does not, we want you to know, Your Majesty, that we will not serve your gods or worship the image of gold you have set up.

In Shadrach, Meshach, and Abednego's response, we learn that worship is not conditional. It is not a mere transaction where we offer praise only when God answers our prayers or provides what we desire.

True worship is rooted in the acknowledgment of God's sovereignty and goodness, regardless of our circumstances or the outcomes we experience in life.

These men understood that God's character was not defined by their present situation, and they were unwavering in their commitment to stand firm in that truth, even when it meant facing the ultimate cost—their lives.

Their praise wasn't rooted in the hope of deliverance, but in their unshakable belief in the nature of a faithful and all-powerful God who is worthy of worship at all times.

This presents a profound challenge for all of us—worshiping God not because of what He gives us, but because He is inherently worthy of our praise simply because of who He is.

Our praise should not be swayed by our feelings, the specific outcomes of our prayers, or the fluctuating seasons of life. We are called to praise God in the storms, in the silence, and in the waiting—not because we understand what He is doing, but because He is always worthy, unchanging and faithful in every circumstance.

When we truly grasp that our relationship with God is not a means to an end, but a continual, steadfast connection with a God who is constant and eternal, our worship transforms. It becomes more than just a reaction to what we experience; it evolves into a declaration of trust, no matter what we see or feel in the moment.

Our worship becomes a bold statement of faith: "Even if You don't, You are still good; even if I don't understand, You are still sovereign." This deep, unwavering faith allows us to honor God not just for what He does, but for who He is—a God whose goodness, power, and love transcend the highs and lows of our lives.

Reflection Questions:

1. Have you ever found yourself tempted to praise God only when things are going well or when you get the answer you expect?

What does that reveal about your understanding of who God is?

2. In what areas of your life have you been tying your worship to God's actions rather than His character? How can you begin to shift from a transactional view of faith to a relationship-based view, where worship is a response to who God is, not just what He does?

3. If you were stripped of everything—your health, your wealth, your security—would your worship of God remain unwavering? Why or why not? What does your answer reveal about where you place your ultimate trust and value?

4. When considering the idea that worship is about God's character and not our circumstances, how does this shift your perspective on your current struggles? How can you start choosing to praise God for who He is, even if your circumstances haven't changed?

She hadn't cried in a long time, but here she was, crying.

She thought she was strong, thought she could handle anything—even losing her dad.

She couldn't let her siblings see her weak, not now, not ever.

She had to stand strong for them. But somewhere along the way, she forgot that she needed to be strong for herself, too.

The tears stung her eyes as they fell, and the ache in her chest grew, twisting her stomach.

It felt like she might shatter, with no one to feel the loss but her.

If she could just disappear, she thought, maybe she'd see him again.

Maybe he'd tell her he was proud, that he was watching over her, that he didn't want her with him—not yet.

He'd want her to live her life, to make him even prouder.

Closing her eyes, she felt ready to let go, to leave the pain behind.

She wanted the suffering to end, to see her papa again.

As she drifted to sleep, she hoped he'd be there when she woke, and that somehow, the pain would finally be gone.

XV.

I'd lost people before. My father's death wasn't the first, but the scar it left was deep, unmistakable. Sometimes I imagined that if someone could open my heart, they'd see the brokenness laid bare, visible for all to see. Grief wasn't a feeling I was unfamiliar with, but this time, it lingered, heavy and suffocating. It left a bitter taste in my mouth, and even now, I feel as though I've been traumatized by it.

I had believed, naively, that grief was linear. That I could move through the stages one after the other, and eventually come out on the other side. I thought it would be neat, orderly. How wrong I was. It was messy, confusing, unpredictable, a storm that I could never have fully prepared for. In the wake of my father's passing, I became overprotective. I hovered over my family, constantly calling, checking in, making sure everyone was okay. In every prayer, I named them all, one by one, praying for their safety, for their lives to be long and shielded from harm. But at the same time, I started to withdraw. I'd pull away from relationships, sometimes intentionally, sometimes not, as if my heart were playing a cruel game of hide and seek. The fear of losing someone else gripped me, made me retreat. If I stayed distant, perhaps I could protect myself from that pain again. Perhaps if I loved less, I would hurt less.

I hated grief. Hated it with a passion I didn't know I was capable of. The pain was unbearable at times, to the point where I questioned my sanity. How could something hurt so much? I had known heartache before—broken friendships, goodbyes to people and places I loved—but nothing had prepared me for this. This was deeper. It felt like a part of my soul had been ripped away, leaving me raw, bleeding, struggling to breathe.

One night, I lay awake, as I had for so many nights before. Sleep had become a distant memory, and insomnia, a relentless companion. It had worsened since my father's death, and nothing, not even the comfort of chamomile tea, could quiet the storm inside me. I hadn't taken sleeping pills; I never liked them. So, I endured the nights, exhausted but unable to rest. That night, though, I was beyond tired. I was weary. As I lay there, staring into the darkness, I felt something stir within me, a desperate need to reach out to God, and the only thing I could think to do was pray. So, I whispered into the stillness,

"Father, I can't do this anymore. I feel like this pain is sucking the life out of me. If You don't save me, if You don't help me, what hope do I have? Could You just let me sleep? Please, let me close my eyes and sleep—just once."

That prayer wasn't just a plea for sleep; it was a cry for rescue. I needed God to intervene, to take the weight off my chest, to silence the constant ache in my heart. I had prayed before, but this felt different. This time, I was fully surrendering, laying my pain at His feet because I had nothing left to hold on to.

I had always dreaded the night. In the darkness, grief felt heavier. Everyone was asleep, and I was left alone with my sorrow. During the day, I could escape to the park, near the Philadelphia museum, where children played, and people laughed. I could pretend life was still normal. But at night, reality hit me hard.

The silence was deafening, and my grief became a suffocating presence. But that night, after my prayer, something shifted. It was subtle at first, but unmistakable. As I lay there, too exhausted to cry anymore, I felt the weight that had been crushing my chest lift.

The pain that had been so relentless began to ease. It was as though God had heard me and responded immediately. I felt something I hadn't felt in months—a peace that went deeper than just a feeling.

It was as if God Himself had wrapped His arms around me, and in that embrace, the turmoil within me stilled. It wasn't just that I felt better—I felt held, cared for, loved in a way that words can't fully describe. The tears stopped, and for the first time in what felt like forever, I didn't feel broken anymore. There was no dread, no fear. The next thing I knew, I was drifting into sleep, something that had eluded me for so long.

When I woke, the morning light felt different. It wasn't just the fact that I had slept through the night—it was the peace I carried with me. I had slept deeply, yes, but more than that, I had been restored.

God had given me rest, not just for my body, but for my soul. I knew, in that moment, that He had been with me, right there in the middle of my pain. He hadn't abandoned me, and that realization flooded me with a joy I hadn't felt in a long time.

I've never love to ask "Why?" when things go wrong. Maybe it's because I'm more focused on finding solutions than dwelling on questions that might never have answers. But sometimes, life brings moments when you can't help but ask. Why did God take my father? Why does He do the things He does—things we can't even begin to understand?

I don't have those answers. But what comforts me, what brings me peace, is knowing that God doesn't just do things and leave us to deal with the fallout alone. He is with us—every step, in every tear, in every sleepless night. He doesn't abandon us in the fire; He walks through it with us. And that truth brings me more joy than I can express.

The next day, I slept again, but I remember waking up from a strange dream—too long to explain here—but I remember waking with a heaviness in my heart. Every failure, every hardship, every loss came rushing back to me yet again, weighing me down before I even stepped out of bed.

But then, I heard a voice, clear as day, say, "*I will carry you through.*" The voice was so strong, so audible, that I couldn't ignore it. Throughout the day, it echoed in my mind, and every time I heard it, it brought with it a level of peace I could neither explain nor understand. For the first time, I had to force myself to worry. My life was complete disarray. how could I possibly have such peace? It didn't make sense. But the peace kept winning, overcoming every anxious thought I tried to hold on to. It overwhelmed me so completely that I felt almost ridiculous for trying so hard to stress. That was the beginning—at least on my part—of a new journey. A journey where I was ready to let God take the wheel.

Psalm 55:22

Throw your burden upon the LORD, and he will sustain you. He will never allow the godly to be upended

God calls us to cast our burdens on Him, especially when life feels unbearable. When the weight of our struggles threatens to crush us, we often feel tempted to run from the pain, seeking temporary escapes in distractions, substances, or fleeting moments of relief. These distractions may provide momentary respite, but they can never offer the true healing our hearts long for. In those moments of overwhelming hardship, it's only God who can truly sustain us. He is our refuge and strength, an ever-present help in trouble. When we reach the end of ourselves, when we're physically and emotionally exhausted and the world feels too heavy to carry, He is there, steadfast and unchanging, to uphold us with His mighty hand. Surrendering our burdens to Him doesn't mean our struggles will instantly disappear, but it does mean we are no longer carrying them alone. God's faithfulness is unwavering; He doesn't leave us in our trials, even when the storm seems endless. He has been by our side all along, steadying us through every trial, every sleepless night, and every moment of confusion when the path forward seems unclear. Even in the darkest moments, when we feel empty, lost, or broken, we can trust in His promise: He will never let us fall. Just as He binds up our wounds and restores our broken hearts, He holds us firmly, His loving arms a refuge we can lean into. In our surrender, He invites us to release the things we cannot bear on our own, reminding us that His yoke is easy, and His burden is light. When we cast our cares on Him, we find peace that surpasses understanding, strength to continue the journey, and the assurance that He is working in ways we may not see, but we can trust are for our good. Even when the answers don't come right away, He is weaving a plan of healing and restoration, and in His perfect timing, all things will be made new.

Reflection questions:

1. When life becomes overwhelming and the weight of your struggles feels unbearable, do you find yourself trying to carry the burden on your own, or do you instinctively turn to God for help? What do you think influences that response?

2. Reflecting on the promise that God will never let you fall, how does this truth impact your understanding of His unwavering faithfulness, especially during difficult times? In what ways does this promise provide peace and assurance, even when circumstances seem chaotic or uncertain? How can you remind yourself of this truth when you're facing challenges?

3. Think of a time when you reached the end of yourself—when you were physically, emotionally, or spiritually drained. How did God show up to support and sustain you during that season? What did you learn from that experience about His constant presence in your life, and how can you carry that understanding into future struggles?

4. Are there any burdens or struggles you're still holding onto that you haven't fully surrendered to God? What do you think might be preventing you from releasing them into His care, and how can you begin to trust Him more fully with those parts of your life? In seasons of emptiness or confusion, how can you remind yourself that God's promise to never let you fall remains true, and how can this truth shape your response to future challenges?

You always give more than I ask for.

In your infinite wisdom and boundless love, you ask me to trust you, to place my faith in your hands. You ask me to open my heart to the depths of your affection.

You ask me to give you my heart, to surrender wholly to you, and in return, you give me life itself. You provide for me in ways I could never have imagined.

When I am in need, you are there with exactly what I require, often before I even realize it myself.

You keep my heart alive, breathing new hope and joy into every beat. You sustain me through every challenge, guiding me with your steady hand and unwavering presence.

Beyond everything I could ever ask or think, you give me more than I deserve.

Your generosity knows no bounds, and your love surpasses all understanding.

Every day, you shower me with blessings, with gifts that I could never earn but are freely given.

You fill my life with beauty, wonder, and grace, constantly reminding me of your unfailing devotion. In you, I find my greatest treasure. Your love is a sanctuary, a place of peace and fulfillment. With you, my heart is always full, my spirit always lifted. For all you have given and all you continue to give, I am forever grateful. Your love is the greatest gift of all, a blessing beyond measure,

a testament to the incredible goodness that you are.

XVI.

I remember the last time I faced the suffocating grip of depression and suicidal thoughts. It was a regular weekend day in Wichita, Kansas. I was taking a bath, letting the warmth envelop me like a cocoon, when I suddenly heard a whisper in my spirit: "Do you know that God has called you for something grand?" At first, I shrugged it off, thinking, "Yeah, sure." But the voice persisted, gently urging me: "There is a call on your life, and God has invested so much in you."

These are phrases most Christians hear; we hear them often yet believing them for ourselves can feel impossible. I couldn't fathom how I was meant to fulfill this purpose, whatever that purpose was, with the weight of my struggles looming over me. How could I chase after something grand when I was constantly drowning in depression, grappling with the darkness that whispered I wasn't enough? What about grief and the weight that it brought? What about all the things in my life that were not perfect yet? my life was all over the place. I could not even begin to Consider it.

The thought of pursuing my calling felt insurmountable, as if I were climbing a mountain with no summit in sight, each step a struggle against the invisible weight pressing down on my shoulders.

In that moment, my mind raced with self-doubt. I thought of all the times I had fallen short, the moments of despair that had painted my world gray. Memories of past failures replayed in my mind, each one like a heavy stone added to the burden I carried. The burden of expectations—both from myself and others—felt like a suffocating shroud that stifled any spark of ambition.

I tried to ignore the voice with all my strength, but it kept repeating, each iteration melting my heart a little more; it was as if my heart had always longed for confirmation that my life had meaning, that there was still hope.

In that fleeting moment of clarity, I felt a shift; I began to pray, pouring out my heart to God. I laid bare the tragedies of my life, recounting the times I felt abandoned by joy, the heavy cloak of depression that had become my constant companion, and the question that haunted me: How could I possibly fulfill the grand purpose He was calling me to when the fog of despair enveloped me so tightly? Each word I spoke felt like a release, yet I was acutely aware of the storm still swirling around me.

Then came the reply: "The battle is not yours; it has never been yours. The battle is Mine." The softness of that voice, the comfort it brought, pierced through my anguish. It was a reminder that I didn't have to fight this fight alone. As those words washed over me, tears flowed freely, a cathartic release of pent-up frustration and sorrow. I had never experienced such profound solace; it was as if a weight had been lifted so suddenly it startled me. That moment felt like a release akin to instinctively pulling one's hand away from something scalding hot.

Joy bubbled up inside me, an unexplainable laughter escaping my lips. I realized, in that instant, I had just encountered the last battle I would face against depression and suicidal thoughts. I felt free, alive—this was a sweetness, a lightness that felt almost surreal. I could envision a bright horizon stretching out before me, filled with possibilities I hadn't dared to dream of.

The laughter was unexpected, but it felt genuine, bubbling from a place deep within me that had been silenced for too long. Although I wasn't leaping with excitement for life just yet, something profound had shifted. I was no longer crippled by despair, and that realization was monumental. Yet, I knew freedom wasn't a destination; it was a journey. Life doesn't simply pause at the point of release. I had to actively walk out that freedom, step by step, navigating the terrain of my thoughts and emotions.

While I still grappled with many questions, I could now seek answers with a heart that was beginning to heal. Hope blossomed where deep sadness once resided, replaced by ideas, possibilities, and dreams that I was still learning to navigate. I began to recognize that each day was a chance to discover new facets of myself, new passions to pursue, and a renewed sense of purpose.

This is my story, and I don't want it to overshadow the reality of depression. I struggled for years, researching and trying to understand the depths of mental health. I had learned along the way that Depression didn't always stem from life's traumas; sometimes, it was rooted in chemical imbalances and other complex factors.

In my culture, mental health often goes unspoken, leaving many to cope in silence. I faced the stigma of seeking help, feeling like a failure for not being able to manage my struggles alone, especially within the context of African stereotypes that deny mental illness. The notion that "Africans don't suffer from such things" loomed heavily over me, making me question my own experiences and validity.

To anyone out there facing similar battles: don't hesitate to seek professional help. You are not alone, and seeking support doesn't make you a failure, regardless of where you come from. My hope is that one day, the conversation around mental health will open up in my community and beyond, allowing others to share their stories without fear. In the end, healing is a journey, and it's one we can walk together, shedding light on the shadows of mental health. Together, we can create a space where vulnerability is celebrated and healing is embraced, fostering a community that understands and uplifts one another.

A Little Extra:

Around the same time, God began working on my perception of myself. "You are fearfully and wonderfully made," (Psalm 139:14) the words echoed in my mind, repeating over and over. I can't even remember exactly how I first stumbled upon that verse. It was something my dad had preached about, something I had heard countless times before. But this time, it hit me in a way I had never experienced. It felt as if I were hearing it for the first time. My eyes seemed newly opened to its depth, and in that moment, something shifted deep within me. That verse wasn't just a line of scripture anymore—it felt alive, like it was speaking directly to me. I began to repeat it to myself, though shyly at first. It felt strange, awkward even, but those words rang so true that my heart couldn't deny them. With a sense of quiet determination, I went and stood in front of the mirror, repeating the verse softly, my eyes closed. Then I opened my eyes, bracing myself to see the reflection. And do you know what I saw staring back at me?

Can you guess?

No, it wasn't Jesus, ha.

It was a beautiful person. I saw my own reflection, and for the first time, I thought, "*I am beautiful.*" I couldn't believe I had never seen myself that way before. I began to touch every part of my face, every feature I had once disliked—each one was beautiful. My nose, my cheeks, my lips—oh, how beautiful they were. It was as though I was seeing myself for the first time, truly seeing myself, without the harsh filter of self-criticism that had clouded my vision for so long. I couldn't believe I had ever hated myself.

I remembered the days when I would look into the mirror and feel nothing but disgust. The reflection staring back at me felt foreign, like an enemy I couldn't escape. I searched for something—anything—within myself that was worth loving, but all I found were cracks, flaws, and broken pieces. I was lost, overwhelmed by a fog of confusion and shame. I wished I could just disappear, convinced that the world would be better off without me—or perhaps, that no one would even notice if I were gone.

But then God stepped in. His love came like a sudden, piercing light, breaking through the darkness I had been drowning in.

I prayed to God, saying,

> *"You created me well, and I am so sorry I ever hated myself."*

As I said those words, I felt His love fill my heart so profoundly, I couldn't help but let a tear fall. The love He showed me is beyond my understanding. It's tender yet relentless, like waves that gradually shape and smooth the roughest stones. I pause, I reflect, and I realize that His love for me is boundless and unshakeable. How could He see value in me when I couldn't even see it in myself? Yet, there it was—His love for me, always constant, never wavering.

God gently, but persistently, reminded me that I am fearfully and wonderfully made. He whispered my worth back to me until the lies faded and the truth began to take root in my soul. He never grew weary of pursuing me, even when I turned away. He wrapped me in His love and reminded me that I am His masterpiece—crafted with care, purpose, and intention. He called me good and worthy, even when I couldn't see it. He told me I am loved—deeply and without condition—until I finally began to believe it.

That verse, "You are fearfully and wonderfully made," became more than just words to me. It became the truth that healed the brokenness inside me. And today, I stand in the mirror and say those words with confidence, knowing that I am loved by God, created with infinite value, and beautiful, just as I am.

John 11:43-44

Then Jesus shouted, "Lazarus, come out!". And the dead man came out, his hands and feet bound in graveclothes, his face wrapped in a headcloth. Jesus told them, "Unwrap him and let him go!"

Here, we witness an extraordinary miracle: Jesus, with a simple command, raises Lazarus from the dead. Lazarus, bound in grave clothes and sealed in a tomb for four days, responds to the voice of Jesus and steps out alive. This moment is not only a powerful display of Jesus' divine authority but a vivid illustration of His ability to breathe life into the most hopeless situations.

Lazarus' resurrection is a profound reminder that no matter how deep the darkness or how dead a situation may seem, God's power is greater.

In our own lives, especially during seasons of despair, pain, or hopelessness, it can often feel as though we are buried under the weight of our circumstances.

At times, we may feel spiritually lifeless, disconnected, or even trapped in a tomb of emotional or mental anguish. But just as Jesus called Lazarus out of the grave, He is still calling us to rise. He invites us into a new life, healing, and restoration.

When we feel broken, forgotten, or overwhelmed, Jesus does not leave us there. His voice is the one that has the power to revive us, to renew our hearts and minds, and to bring us into the fullness of His healing.

I can personally testify to the truth of this promise. During my darkest moments, when I felt trapped in a season of depression and hopelessness, it was as if my spirit had been entombed. Yet, just as Jesus called Lazarus by name, I heard His voice gently calling me, lifting me from despair and breathing new life into my soul. It was not instantaneous or without effort, but God's touch was real. This passage assures us that God's healing power is not limited to physical restoration alone. He is also deeply invested in restoring our broken hearts, minds, and spirits.

Reflection Questions:

1. Just as Jesus called Lazarus to come out of the tomb, He calls you to step into new life. What areas of your life feel dead or hopeless right now, and how might you begin to trust God for His miraculous healing in those places?

2. God has the power to heal, even the deepest emotional wounds. When you think about your hardships or struggles, how does it change your perspective to remember that God can bring life and restoration, no matter how long the suffering has lasted?

3. Lazarus came out of the tomb with grave clothes still on. What "grave clothes" — the remnants of your past pain or depression —

do you need to let go of in order to walk fully in the new life God offers?

4. Reflect on a time when you experienced God's healing in an unexpected way. How can this testimony strengthen your faith, especially when facing moments of emotional or mental struggle in the future?

Dear God, My beloved,

I searched for you, but you were the one who found me.

I never knew I could feel this way until your gentle gaze fell upon me.

I was lost, far from my dreams, but you brought me near to yours.

I give you everything, holding nothing back, because nothing is truly mine.

I find my life only when I give it to you.

In your eyes, I saw myself, and suddenly all my doubts faded away.

In that moment, I knew I was loved, despite my flaws.

When you found me, I discovered who I truly am. My love, you've taught me that the greatest gift you could ever give me is yourself.

My treasure

XVII.

The year 2024 stands as the most profound and transformative season of my walk with God—a year that changed not only the way I viewed Him but also the way I understood myself, my purpose, and my faith. It was a year full of lessons, revelations, and moments of both deep joy and deep wrestling.

If only I had known Him in this way all along, I sometimes wonder how much further along I would be in my spiritual journey. How much richer would my faith have been? How many doubts, fears, and unnecessary detours could I have avoided? But I try not to dwell too long on what could have been or what might have been different.

After all, God's timing is always perfect, even when it feels delayed or unclear in the moment. Instead, I make the conscious choice to savor the present and to be fully grateful for the time, the experiences, and the intimacy I now have with Him. This awareness of His presence is a gift I treasure more than words can adequately express.

Still, even in the midst of this incredible spiritual journey, there was one desire—a longing—that seemed to weigh heavier on my heart than almost anything else, even heavier than the pressing need to land a stable job.

That desire was for marriage. It wasn't a fleeting wish or a passing thought; it was a constant prayer, an ever-present yearning that was with me all the time. That desire began to intensify to such a degree that it started to affect my relationship with God in ways I hadn't anticipated.

It felt as though everyone around me—friends, acquaintances, even distant connections—was stepping into marriage and starting families, moving forward into the very season I longed for so desperately. Meanwhile, I felt left behind, stuck in a place of waiting, wondering when—or if—it would ever be my turn. No matter how many times well-meaning people offered words of encouragement like, "It will come in God's timing," or "Your turn is coming," those reassurances often felt hollow. They did little to soothe the ache in my heart or silence the doubts that whispered louder with each passing day.

I couldn't shake the feeling that God's hand was long enough to bless those around me, but somehow not long enough to reach me. It seemed as though He was pouring out His blessings on my friends and loved ones while withholding that same goodness from me. The most challenging moments were when God prompted me to pray for others and their marriages. I would fast, I would pray, and soon after, I would witness God's hand move powerfully in their lives. I would hear their testimonies of answered prayers and see the joy of new beginnings. I was truly happy for them—my faith even grew stronger as I witnessed God's faithfulness—but at the same time, I couldn't escape the quiet sting of being overlooked.

There were times when it felt as though an invisible barrier existed between God's blessings and my own life. It was during these moments of vulnerability and longing that a familiar voice returned to torment me. This was the same voice that had once whispered dark lies, urging me to end my life. Now it carried a new message, one that was equally insidious: "God knows marriage is a good thing, but He's withholding it from you. How can you trust His intentions?"

The argument was compelling, almost too persuasive to resist. If God Himself had established marriage as a holy and good institution, why would He deny it to me? What possible reason could He have for withholding something so deeply rooted in His design? I began to wrestle with these questions, and as I did, resentment quietly crept into my heart. I found myself questioning not only God's timing but also His very character. Why would He ask me to intercede so fervently for others' happiness, to witness His miraculous hand in their lives, yet seemingly close His hand when it came to my own prayers? How could He claim to love me when I felt so overlooked, so forgotten?

My trust in Him faltered, and for a time, my relationship with Him grew shaky. Faith, the very foundation of my walk with Him no longer seemed to be working. The pressures from my culture, which often placed a significant emphasis on marriage, only added to my insecurities. The whispers of doubt grew louder, telling me that maybe something was wrong with me—that perhaps, in some way, I wasn't enough. All these swirling thoughts seemed to conclude in the same painful refrain: "God can, but He won't." And as that lie echoed in my heart, I found myself believing it more and more.

One day, during a particularly raw and honest moment of prayer, I poured out my frustrations to God. I was tired of pretending, tired of holding back my emotions. "God," I cried, "I don't understand. I don't understand why You're withholding this from me. I need a husband!

I stopped praying for a few days after that outburst. I felt drained, disillusioned, and uncertain about how to move forward. Then, during a conversation with one of my closest friends, she shared a story that would pierce me to my core. She told me about a moment when she was worshiping God in the shower, just spending time in His presence. In the midst of her worship, she suddenly heard Him ask her a question that shook her to her very foundation: "If I took your fiancé away, would I still be enough for you?"

Her initial reaction was to laugh nervously, but as the weight of the question sank in, she realized the sobering truth: her answer was no. God was not first in her heart.

As she recounted this experience, I felt an undeniable sting of conviction in my own heart. Her story forced me to confront a question I had been avoiding: Would God still be enough for me if everything I was holding onto—every dream, every desire, every plan I had for my life, etc.—was taken away? Would He still be enough if I never got married at all?

That question humbled me deeply. It revealed the true state of my heart, the misplaced priorities, and the unhealthy weight I had placed on marriage as the ultimate solution to my problems. In that moment of reflection, I realized that marriage had become an idol in my life.

It was time to dethrone that idol and invite God back to His rightful place on the throne of my heart. Around that time, I began reading A.W. Tozer's *The Pursuit of God* with another friend, and one chapter in particular, "The Blessedness of Possessing Nothing," stood out to me. Tozer's words cut through my defenses, speaking directly to the core of my struggles. He wrote about how, in the beginning, God was seated on the throne of our hearts, and our desires were for Him alone. But over time, sin distorted those desires, causing us to crave the gifts of God more than God Himself.

At the end of the chapter, there was a prayer that resonated deeply with me:

> "Father, I want to know Thee, but my cowardly heart fears to give up its toys. I cannot part with them without inward bleeding... I come trembling, but I do come. Please root from my heart all those things which I have cherished so long... so that Thou mayest enter and dwell there without a rival."

As I prayed those words, God began to reveal to me that no man could ever satisfy my soul in the way that He could. All the things I had been searching for—intimacy, fulfillment, identity—were already found in Him. His gentle whisper reminded me, "The answer to your loneliness is Me."

Though my heart was being transformed, I wrestled with how to live it out practically. "God, what does this look like?" I asked. His response was simple yet profound: He called me to immerse myself in His Word. At first, I was confused, feeling that His answer had nothing to do with what I had prayed for. But I chose to trust Him and commit myself to reading His Word. *"Maybe"*, I thought, *"I'll find some answers or direction."*

The more I read, the more layers of misunderstanding and misplaced expectations were peeled away. Slowly but surely, He reshaped my heart, teaching me to trust Him in ways I never had before. And in that quiet obedience, I began to see that the answers I sought were never as important as the deeper, lasting peace that came from simply trusting Him.

Psalm 34:10

Young lions may go hungry or even starve, but if you trust the LORD, you will never miss out on anything good.

This passage serves as a profound reminder of God's unmatched sufficiency and faithfulness: "The lions may grow weak and hungry, but those who seek the Lord lack no good thing." Even lions—the symbol of strength, power, and self-sufficiency—face moments of scarcity. This comparison reveals a beautiful truth: no matter how capable or strong we may appear, our own efforts and resources will never fully sustain us. In contrast, for those who seek the Lord with sincere hearts, there is no lack. God, in His infinite goodness, ensures that we are provided for—not always in the way we expect, but in the ways that matter most for our growth, peace, and purpose.

This verse encourages us to recognize that true provision and fulfillment do not come from what we can earn or achieve but from a relationship with God. When we seek Him, He meets us in our need, not only providing for us physically but also nourishing us emotionally and spiritually. His promise is not limited to material abundance, or even provision for a spouse; it extends to every area of our lives—our peace, our joy, our sense of belonging, and our hope.

Even in seasons of lack or hardship, this promise stands firm. God's faithfulness does not depend on our circumstances. When we trust Him and turn our hearts toward Him, we find that He is more than enough to fill every void, heal every ache, and satisfy every longing. He withholds no good thing from His children, and His provision is always perfect, even when it doesn't align with our expectations. To seek the Lord is to anchor ourselves in the assurance that He sees, knows, and cares for every detail of our lives. When we do, we discover a deep truth: God Himself is the ultimate good, and in Him, we truly lack nothing.

Reflection Questions:

1. Is your relationship with God rooted in a desire for His will, or do you tend to approach Him more for what He can give you? How does your prayer life reflect the balance between seeking God's will and asking for His provision? What specific steps can you take today to focus more on cultivating a relationship with God rather than just asking for His blessings?

2. When you are in a season of waiting, how do you manage the tension between trusting God's timing and longing for answers? What helps you maintain patience and trust when you feel that God is not acting as quickly as you want? How can you actively release your expectations to God and choose to rest in His sovereignty?

3. How do you keep your heart open to God's purposes in times of uncertainty, instead of becoming frustrated or disillusioned? How can you shift your mindset from seeing difficulties as setbacks to viewing them as opportunities for spiritual growth?

4. What specific aspects of God's character can you lean into when life feels challenging or when you are waiting on answers? How can you begin to see your waiting period as a sacred opportunity to become more like Christ, rather than simply a delay?

God, You have been my treasure all along

The past has shown me how fragile and powerless I am, much like a jar of clay, easily broken and vulnerable. But in your love, I have discovered a treasure—a power that is not my own but yours, sustaining me in ways I never imagined. As the Scriptures declare, "We have this treasure in jars of clay to show that this all-surpassing power is from God and not from us. We are hard pressed on every side, but not crushed; perplexed, but not in despair; persecuted; not abandoned; struck down, but not destroyed."

In every storm, in every uncertainty, your love has been my unwavering strength. It is your presence that empowers me, guiding me through the darkest valleys and lifting me above the fiercest trials. You have given me victory, not just in battles I can see, but in ways that transcend my understanding. Your love has opened my eyes to a new perspective, showing me that I am never alone, and that with you, I am equipped to face anything. I am covered by your love, wrapped in the safety of your embrace, and transformed by the deep intimacy we share. Is there anything in this world more valuable than this? To be known by you, loved by you, and strengthened by you—this is the greatest treasure, the most profound gift. Your love has changed everything, and for that, I am eternally grateful.

The past taught me that I am powerless, but your love has taught me that you are my strength and constant force empowering me through every storm and uncertainty. You give me victory in more ways than I can explain you have given me a new perspective and have equipped me with you. I am covered by your love and transformed by your intimacy with me. Is there anything that is more valuable than this

XVIII.

Since 2021, I've developed a habit of asking God for a word for the year—a word that would guide my focus and reveal what He was about to do in my life. Each year, I spend time in prayer, asking God for that word. In 2023, for example, my word was "seek God first," accompanied by the Bible verse Matthew 6:33: *"But seek ye first the kingdom of God and His righteousness, and all these things will be added unto you."* I was so excited about this word and couldn't wait to share it with my friends. But I soon realized that every word from God comes with challenges. My fight became learning how to truly set myself up to seek God first, especially when everything around me was calling for my attention, demanding that I prioritize other things.

At the beginning of 2024, the phrase "abide and be anchored" resonated deeply in my spirit. At first, I didn't fully understand its significance, but it echoed over and over in my mind, much like a persistent whisper that wouldn't go away. So, I prayed for God to reveal its meaning. In response,

He led me to the parable of the Sower in Matthew 13:3-8, 18-23. God showed me that these words were both a command and a prophecy. A command, because I needed to intentionally anchor myself in His Word to strengthen my faith, regardless of the season I was in. A prophecy, because He was speaking over me, promising that as I abided in Him, I would be anchored—unshakable in my faith—no matter the storms or trials I faced.

After reflecting on this passage, it became clear: God was calling me into deeper waters. For much of my Christian life, my faith had been based on how I felt—on my perception of God's goodness, which was often tied to my circumstances. When things were going well, I was at church, reading my Bible, involved in community—doing everything I thought a "good" Christian should do. But when life threw challenges my way, I retreated into rebellion, distancing myself from God because I didn't know how to relate to Him during those times. My relationship with God was inconsistent, fluctuating with the highs and lows of my emotions.

During the year, God's work in me had been to change that. He desires a relationship with me that is not contingent on my feelings or circumstances. He is drawing me into a place of consistency, where intimacy with Him will grow, and my character will be shaped by that relationship. God has shown me that true spiritual growth comes not from avoiding challenges but from remaining anchored in His presence no matter what I face. Through this process, I've fallen deeply in love with Him—a love that brings a wholeness I'd never known before. My soul feels alive in a way it never has, and now I find myself praying that everyone could experience this fullness. For the first time, I am truly anchored—not just in my faith, but in the deep assurance that God is enough, always and forever.

I have come to believe that God has always been enough. He requires no addition, no supplement to His being—He is more than sufficient, and His fullness is beyond anything we could ever imagine. There's a completeness in Him that transcends the desires we often chase after, believing they will bring us wholeness. When you truly encounter His fullness, everything else pales in comparison.. Once I began to experience God's sufficiency, I realized that everything else pales in comparison. In fact, it's not even a matter of comparison, because there is no contest. The things I thought would fill the void in my heart—marriage, success, validation etc.—were not the answer. They matter, but they can't compare to the all-encompassing satisfaction that comes from knowing God.

It's like discovering a treasure so rich and boundless that you wonder why you ever settled for less. What God has been showing me this year is that the answer to my loneliness, my feelings of inadequacy, and my pursuit of something to fill the emptiness is all found in Him. He had been enough all along, but I hadn't fully grasped it until I began abiding in His Word. As I leaned into the truth of His sufficiency, I realized no earthly thing could compare to His presence. My soul, which had been searching for a home, found its rest in God. There's no need for extra because His love, His presence, and His being are more than enough to sustain me, no matter what life brings. This is what it means to be anchored in Him—finding that His fullness leaves no room for lack and that the wholeness He offers is unlike anything this world can give.

This year has been transformative. God has gently and steadfastly called me to a place where I no longer seek satisfaction in the fleeting things of this world. Instead, I find myself learning what it truly means to rest in Him and rely on His sufficiency. No longer am I chasing after what I thought I needed to feel complete. I've discovered that everything I've been searching for was already found in the One who has always been enough.

Matthew 13:44

The Kingdom of Heaven is like a treasure that a man discovered hidden in a field. In his excitement, he hid it again and sold everything he owned to get enough money to buy the field.

Jesus shares a profound parable about the kingdom of heaven, likening it to a treasure hidden in a field. When a man stumbles upon this treasure, he immediately recognizes its immense value—so much so that he joyfully sells everything he owns to buy the field and secure the treasure for himself. The man's actions reveal a deep truth about the nature of God's kingdom: it is priceless, incomparable, and worth any sacrifice. This treasure represents the fullness of God's presence, His unending love, His sufficiency, and the eternal life He offers. It is a gift so extraordinary that it surpasses all the pursuits and possessions of this world.

The parable invites us to reflect on what we truly value and where our hearts are anchored. It challenges us to evaluate whether the things we chase—relationships, success, validation, material wealth—are overshadowing our pursuit of God's kingdom. These pursuits, while not inherently wrong, can never fill the deepest voids within us. They are temporary and often leave us yearning for more. In contrast, God's presence is the only treasure that satisfies completely, meeting every longing and providing lasting fulfillment.

This story also highlights the joy that comes with prioritizing God above all else. The man's decision to sell everything wasn't done begrudgingly; it was fueled by the joyful realization of the treasure's worth. When we grasp the magnitude of what God offers—a relationship with Him, peace that surpasses understanding, and a purpose that transcends earthly achievements—our perspective shifts. The things we once held tightly lose their grip on us because we've found something infinitely greater.

Ultimately, this parable reminds us that God's kingdom isn't just one treasure among many; it is the treasure that redefines everything else. It calls us to seek Him with our whole hearts, trusting that His fullness will meet every need and satisfy every longing in ways that no earthly pursuit ever could

Reflection Questions:

1. Are there specific distractions or idols — such as relationships, ambitions, or possessions — that compete for your attention and affection? How can you begin to release these and make space for God to take center stage in your heart?

2. How often do you find yourself prioritizing your career, achievements, or the approval of others over nurturing your relationship with God? What would it look like to

intentionally put Him first in your daily life?

3. Can you recall a time when God's presence brought you a deeper satisfaction than anything the world could offer? How can you cultivate that sense of joy and fulfillment more consistently in your walk with Him?

4. Are you willing to let go of your most cherished dreams, goals, or possessions if it means embracing the fullness of God's kingdom? What fears or reservations might you need to surrender in order to experience the richness of His presence?

One day, I will look back and see—
You were faithful all along. In the shadows
where doubt crept close,
In the silence that felt unending, You were
there, steady and unseen,
A thread of grace weaving through my chaos.
How many times did I cry out, Believing You
were distant,
When all the while, You carried me?
I searched for answers,
But what You gave me instead was Your
presence—
A quiet assurance, A hand that never let me
fall too far.
Looking back, I see Your fingerprints
On every moment I thought was wasted, On
every path I thought led nowhere.
The prayers I thought You didn't hear Were
seeds You planted in unseen soil,
Growing into a harvest I could not yet
imagine.
How could I not lift my hands in gratitude?

You were faithful when I was faithless. You were steadfast when I was shaken.
Even in the waiting, even in the breaking, You were writing a story of redemption
Too beautiful for me to comprehend.
And so, even now, as I walk through the unknown,
I will whisper thanks for what I cannot yet see.
For one day, I will look back and know— You were faithful.
You were always faithful.

XIX.

One of the most profound lessons I've learned through all these experiences is that Christianity isn't about reaching a final destination, as I once thought. It's not a matter of saying, "I'm saved, and that's it." Instead, it's a lifelong journey—a winding, often challenging road of growing in intimacy with God, being molded into who He's called us to be, and everything that happens in between. I think that's why it's called a "walk with God." It's ongoing, dynamic, and filled with moments that stretch our faith and shape our character. One verse I believes captures this idea is **Hebrews 12:1-2**, which says:

"Therefore, since we are surrounded by such a huge crowd of witnesses to the life of faith, let us strip off every weight that slows us down, especially the sin that so easily trips us up. And let us run with endurance the race God has set before us. We do this by keeping our eyes on Jesus, the champion who initiates and

perfects our faith. Because of the joy awaiting him, he endured the cross, disregarding its shame. Now he is seated in the place of honor beside God's throne."

Another Version says:

"Do you see what this means — all these pioneers who blazed the way, all these veterans cheering us on? It means we'd better get on with it. Strip down, start running — and never quit! No extra spiritual fat, no parasitic sins. Keep your eyes on Jesus, who both began and finished this race we're in. Study how he did it. Because he never lost sight of where he was headed — that exhilarating finish in and with God — he could put up with anything along the way: Cross, shame, whatever. And now he's there, in the place of honor, right alongside God."

This verse shows us that the path we walk is rarely straight or smooth. It's full of unexpected turns, moments of uncertainty, and times when we wonder if God really knows what He's doing.

There are days when we feel we need to take control, to steer our lives in a direction that feels safer or more predictable. We get this false sense of confidence that we know what's best for ourselves, without realizing how limited our perspective really is. We want to sit in the driver's seat of our lives, thinking that we can navigate the journey better than God. But the truth is, most of the time we don't even know where we're going. We may see only a short stretch of the road ahead, while God sees the entire journey, beginning to end.

However, once we learn to trust the true Driver of our lives—once we believe in His goodness, His perfect timing, and His unshakable characters. something profound happens. We begin to let go of the urge to control and instead rest in His sovereignty. We start to see that even when the road seems treacherous, God is guiding us with purpose. It's like Jesus, asleep at the bottom of the boat during a raging storm. The disciples were in a panic, afraid for their lives, while Jesus rested peacefully, fully confident in His Father's control.

In our case, it's as though we're passengers in a car on a winding, turbulent road. The winds might howl, the storm might rage, but instead of gripping the wheel in fear, we can lean back and rest, knowing that the One who's driving sees the entire route and knows exactly how to get us safely to our destination.

I used to believe that being saved was the end goal, the finish line. But now I understand that salvation is only the beginning. There's so much more beyond that initial moment of grace—there's the lifelong process of sanctification, of being refined and transformed by God. And that transformation doesn't come easy. It often happens in seasons of pruning, where God strips away things in our lives that don't align with His will. And in those times, it can feel like God is silent or distant. We might wonder why He seems absent just when we need

Him most. But I've learned that in those quiet, difficult seasons, God is calling us into something deeper. He's inviting us to move beyond our reliance on what we feel, what we think we need, or even what we think we deserve. He's shifting our focus from our circumstances to His unchanging nature.

It's in these refining moments that we learn to build our faith not on the comfort of our situation, but on the unshakable reality of who God is—His faithfulness, His goodness, and His love for us. God's plan for our lives is never as simple as we imagine. It's not just about reaching heaven; it's about who we become along the way. He is constantly working in us and through us, pruning away the parts of our character that don't reflect His heart, while strengthening our faith in the process.

This journey with God is about growth, transformation, and deepening intimacy. It's about becoming more like Him as we walk through life's ups and downs, learning to trust Him more fully with each step.

He refines us, not to break us, but to bring out the purity of faith that trusts Him above all else. And that process—sanctification—is ongoing. It's not a one-time event but a continuous shaping of our hearts and minds into His image. In the moments when He seems quiet or distant, He is often drawing us closer. He's teaching us to rely on Him, not on our emotions or fleeting feelings, but on the truth of who He is. It's easy to trust God when things are going well, but it's in the hardest times that our faith is tested and deepened.

When we're stripped of comfort and control, we find ourselves with no choice but to lean into God, to trust that He is still good, still present, and still guiding us, even when we can't see the full picture. The more we walk with Him, the more we realize that the journey is about so much more than arriving at a destination. It's about learning to trust the One who holds the map, to rest in His sovereignty, and to grow in love and faith even when the road is rough.

Just like Jesus could sleep through the storm because He trusted the Father completely (Matthew 8:23-27), we too can find peace in the midst of chaos when we learn to trust the Driver of our lives. God knows what He's doing, and He's taking us somewhere far greater than we could ever imagine.

Ultimately, this walk with God isn't about reaching a place of comfort or ease. It's about becoming who He's called us to be, about building a relationship with Him that's unshakable. And while the road may be difficult, it's the journey itself—the growth, the trust, the intimacy with God—that shapes us and reveals His glory in our lives. The bumps and twists in the road are not signs of abandonment, but of God's careful, purposeful hand, guiding us closer to Him, refining us, and preparing us for the fullness of His promises.

Philippians 1:6

And so I am sure that God, who began this good work in you, will carry it on until it is finished on the Day of Christ Jesus.

This passage reminds us that our journey with God is not a race to achieve instant perfection but a beautifully intricate process—a continuous, intentional work that He is faithfully carrying out in each of us. This promise is deeply reassuring because it shifts the focus from our own efforts to His unwavering commitment to us. God, who began a good work in us, will not abandon it midway. Instead, He carefully and lovingly refines us, shaping us into the people He designed us to be.

Whether we find ourselves in a season of rapid growth, painful struggle, or quiet stillness, every phase of our journey has purpose. In seasons of growth, God stretches us to reach new heights. In seasons of struggle, He refines us through challenges, teaching us resilience, patience, and trust. And in seasons of stillness, He nurtures our inner being, drawing us closer to His heart. Even the bumps and detours along the way — those moments we might label as setbacks — are part of His masterful plan, tools He uses to mold us more into His image.

Though we may not always see or understand the end result, Philippians 1:6 encourages us to trust the process and the One who is at work within us. Our role is not to perfect ourselves but to remain open to His shaping hand, to trust that He is using every joy, every sorrow, and every waiting season to weave a masterpiece. We can live in confidence, knowing that the good work He began in us is not only ongoing but guaranteed to be completed in His perfect time.

Reflection Questions:

1. When faced with difficulties or unanswered prayers, are you able to rest in the assurance that God's timing and plan are perfect? Or do you find yourself doubting or taking control? How can you learn to trust His unseen work in your heart?

2. What does true commitment to God look like for you? Is your relationship with Him something that you tend to "put on pause" during challenging times, or are you consistently seeking to grow closer to Him in every season? Is there something you're clinging to that you feel you cannot surrender to Him?

3. What are the areas where you feel distant from God, and why do you think that is? What do you think you need to do in order to draw closer to Him?

4. What does it mean to you that God's good work isn't just about what you do but who you are becoming? How can you embrace His ongoing work in your heart, knowing that He is faithful to bring you to completion in His perfect timing?

XX.

Throughout my journey, I have experienced countless moments of joy, pain, growth, and reflection. There were times when God showed up right away, and there were times where he let me sit with the pain and only promised his presence.

There were also times when he showed up in unexpected places and through unexpected people. In those moments when I thought I would actually collapse, he held my hand and said he would carry me through, and that he did.

As I prepare to conclude these lines, I want to share with you four profound truths I have learned. There may be more truths yet to discover, but for where I stand now, these are the lessons that have shaped my heart and my life.

<u>The First Truth</u>: **God is always there**.

If we pause, look around, and truly engage our senses—if we open our hearts to believe—we will find that God is everywhere. In the rustling of the leaves, the warmth of the sun on our skin, the laughter of loved ones, and even in moments of silence, He is present. There is never a moment when He is not near.

Yet, there are times when we may feel He is distant. More often than not, if He seems far away, it is not because He has left us but because we have wandered from Him. Even then, His arms remain open, always ready to draw us back.

The Second Truth: **Life is a mix of challenges and blessings**.

We will face trials; difficulties that may test our faith and stretch our endurance. Being aware of this truth helps us not to be shaken when hardships arise. At the same time, we will also experience moments of abundance and joy, times when life feels full and beautiful.

Both seasons are gifts, and in both, God is at work. He is the One who gives and takes away, yet always with a purpose: to shape us, strengthen us, and draw us closer to Him. Whether in struggle or celebration, we can trust that God is working all things together for our good.

The Third Truth: **We were created with emotions, and we need to embrace them.**

If you are anything like me, you may have a tendency to avoid your emotions—pushing them aside or pretending they don't exist, hoping they'll eventually disappear. But they don't.
Ignoring our feelings only causes them to fester, creating wounds that affect not just our hearts but our minds, bodies, and relationships.
There is a saying that has stuck with me: "When grief comes and knocks at your door, let it in. Allow it to do what it came to do, and then let it go." This saying reminds us that emotions, especially difficult ones, are not our enemies. They come to serve us, to help us relate and make sense of our circumstances and provide insight into how we perceive and process events and help us navigate through life's valleys.

acknowledging and processing them, we make space for growth and peace.

The Fourth and Final Truth: **There is always hope and light at the end of the tunnel.**

The Bible reminds us, "Weeping may endure for a night, but joy comes in the morning" (Psalm 30:5). Even when the night feels endless and the darkness seems overwhelming, the promise of dawn remains. This is a truth that has carried me through my hardest days. No matter how deep the valley or how long the storm, God's light will break through, bringing hope, renewal, and peace.

One Prayer I Want To Leave With You Though, Is This One,

Father,

Come to my rescue. My heart aches with a pain that words cannot fully express, and I am left hollow, consumed by an unrelenting emptiness. There is a longing inside me, a desire so deep it feels like the very core of my being cries out for something I cannot name.

My heart yearns, it craves, it stretches toward things that promise satisfaction, yet those promises are never fulfilled. Instead of peace, I am left lost, wandering through shadows, clutching at illusions that slip through my fingers like sand.

In my emptiness, I run. I flee from the silence where my soul whispers for You. I run from my pain, from my fear, from the truth of what I need most. But instead of running to You, I run to other things. I seek refuge in distractions, in fleeting pleasures, in pursuits that cannot sustain me.

These things — false idols I create in my desperation — pull me further from You. They offer momentary comfort, but they do not heal. Instead, they tighten around me like chains, binding me to a cycle of longing and despair.

Father, I confess my hostility toward You. When my desires are unmet, I grow bitter. I blame You, even as I push You away. My pride blinds me; my selfishness consumes me. And in this cycle of rebellion and regret, I grow weary.

I no longer want to live like this. I no longer want to run from the only One who can truly fill this void within me.

Rescue me, Father. Rescue me from myself. Do not let me seek fulfillment in what will only leave me more broken. Draw me away from the things that steal my soul and shatter my spirit.

Free me from the lust that has taken root in my heart, from the selfish desires that have become my master. Empty me of myself, Father. Strip away my pride, my bitterness, my rebellion — everything that separates me from You. I long to be filled with Your presence, Your love, and Your peace.

Restore me, Father. Breathe life back into this weary soul. Let Your life, the life that is Jesus, fill the emptiness within me. Let His light break through the darkness that has clouded my heart for so long. Remind me of the peace I once knew — the peace that can only be found in You. I feel so far from it now, so far from

You. But I believe You are near, waiting for me to call out.

Show me the way, Father. Guide my steps so they lead me back to You. Let Your truth be my compass, Your love be my anchor. Help me recognize the chains I have forged for myself — the chains of lust, of pride, of idolatry.

Break them, Père. Free me from their hold so I can walk in the freedom only You can give. Let me taste the joy of living in Your presence, the joy of being fully known and fully loved by You.

I am lost, Father. I am drowning in my selfishness, in my misplaced desires, in the chaos of my own making. I have allowed lust to take the throne of my heart, dictating every step I take. I hate what I have become, but I feel powerless to change it on my own. I need You. I need Your strength to overcome what I cannot.

Father, rescue me. Tear down the walls I have built around my heart. Fill the emptiness within me with Your Spirit, with Your life-giving presence.

Remind me that I was made for more than this, that You have a purpose for me that goes beyond my brokenness. Restore to me the joy of salvation, the peace of surrender, the hope of redemption.

I do not want to live like this anymore. I do not want to be ruled by the things that destroy me. I do not want to chase after shadows when You are the light.

Come to my rescue, Father. Lift me out of this pit and set my feet on solid ground. Show me the beauty of living a life fully surrendered to You.

Father, I give You my heart, my broken, wounded, wandering heart. Take it and make it Yours. Teach me to love You above all else, to trust You even when my desires are unmet, to run to You instead of away from You. Lead me back to Your peace, the peace that surpasses all understanding.

Come, Father. Rescue me. Restore me. Make me whole.

In Jesus' name I Pray

Amen!

This conclude our journey through this book.

Thank you faithful readers; it has been a pleasure writing to you.

Until next time.

Notes From The Author

Dear reader,

Thank you for walking this journey with me. Writing these lines has been a deeply personal and transformative experience, and I feel so blessed to share them with you. If you have made it to the end, know that I am grateful for your presence here.

My hope is that these reflections have blessed you as much as, or perhaps even more than, they have blessed me in writing them. This is not the end—it is a new beginning. I would love to hear your thoughts and how these words have impacted your journey. Until then, may God's love, grace, and truth carry you through whatever lies ahead.

With all my heart,

Sincerely,

Your Author

Notes:

The Bible, *Amplified Version*. John 16:33

    I.

The Passion of the Christ. Directed by Mel Gibson, Icon Productions, 2004

The Holy Bible, *Amplified Bible*. Romans 8:28

    II.

The Holy Bible, *New Living Translation*. 1 Peter 2:9

    III.

The Holy Bible, *God's Word Translation*. Psalm 139:13-16

    IV.

The Holy Bible, *Contemporary English Version*. Ecclesiastes 4:1

The Holy Bible, *Berean Study Bible*. Ecclesiastes 4:1

    V.

Seamands, David A. *Healing of Damaged Emotions*. Regal Books, 1991

The Holy Bible, *Good News Translation*. Psalm 34:18

The Holy Bible, *International Standard Version*. Psalm 34:18

(Note: I thought to include two translations because I believe these two capture different perspectives of the same passage, which will provide a broader understanding to the reader.)

    VI.

Every Nation Campus. *Every Nation Campus Website*. Accessed January 16, 2025. www.everynationcampus.org.

The Holy Bible, *Good News Translation*. Matthew 18:21-35

    VII.

The Holy Bible, *Amplified Bible*. 1 John 1:7-9

    VIII.

The Holy Bible, *New Living Translation*. Exodus 34:14

The Holy Bible, *Contemporary English Version*. Psalm 42

IX.

The Holy Bible, *New Living Translation*. Exodus 20:3-6

X.

The Holy Bible, *Contemporary English Version*. Job 1:21

XI.

The Holy Bible, *World English Bible*. Isaiah 41:10

XII.

The Holy Bible, *New Living Translation*. Matthew 11:28-30

XIII.

The Holy Bible, God's Word Translation. Psalm 62:5-6

XIV.

Bethel Music. Goodness of God. *From the album Victory, released February 2019.* Bethel Music Publishing.

The Holy Bible. *Job Chapter 1 (Various translations available, e.g., New Living Translation, King James Version, etc.)*

The Holy Bible, *God's Word Translation*. Daniel 3:17-18

XV.

The Holy Bible, *NET Bible*. Psalm 55:22

XVI.

The Holy Bible, *New Living Translation*. 2 Chronicles 20:15

The Holy Bible, *English Standard Version*. Psalm 139:14

The Holy Bible, *New Living Translation*. John 11:43-44

XVII.

Tozer, A.W. *The Pursuit of God*. Christian Publications, 1948. Chapter 2: *The Blessedness of Possessing Nothing*.

The Holy Bible, *Contemporary English Version*. Psalm 34:10

XVIII.

The Holy Bible, *New International Version*.
Matthew 6:33

The Holy Bible, *New International Version*.
Matthew 13:5-8

The Holy Bible, *New International Version*.
Matthew 18:23

The Holy Bible, *New Living Translation*.
Matthew 13:44

XIX.

The Holy Bible, *Message Version*. Hebrew 12:1-2

The Holy Bible, *New Living Translation*. Hebrew 12:1-2

Note: I thought to include two translations because I believe these two capture different perspectives of the same passage, which will provide a broader understanding to the reader.)

The Holy Bible, *English Standard Version*.
Matthew 8:23-27

The Holy Bible, *Good News Translation*.
Philippians 1:6

XX.

The Holy Bible, *Amplified Bible*. Matthew 28:20

The Holy Bible, *Weymouth New Testament*. John 13:33

The Holy Bible, *Amplified Bible*. Romans 8:28

The Holy Bible, *Good News Translation*. Ephesians 4:26

Beck, M. (n.d.). *When grief comes and knocks at your door, let it in. Allow it to do what it came to do, and then let it go.*

(Note: This quote has been widely paraphrased and attributed to various authors, but its essence aligns with wisdom found in works on emotional healing.)

The Holy Bible, *Holman Christian Standard Bible*. Psalm 30:5

Made in the USA
Middletown, DE
10 February 2025